Good Sex

Also by Gary F. Kelly:

Learning about Sex: The Contemporary Guide
for Young Adults

Sexuality—The Human Perspective

The Healthy Man's Guide

Gary F. Kelly

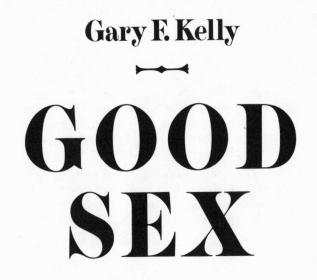

GOOD
SEX

to Sexual Fulfillment

Harcourt Brace Jovanovich

New York and London

Requests for permission to make copies
of any part of the work should be mailed to:
Permissions, Harcourt Brace Jovanovich, Inc.
757 Third Avenue, New York, N.Y. 10017

Printed in the United States of America

Library of Congress Cataloging in Publication Data

Kelly, Gary F
Good sex.

Bibliography: p.
Includes index.
1. Sex instruction for youth. 2. Sex instruction for men.
I. Title.
HQ35.2.K44   301.41′8′024041   78-22257
ISBN 0-15-136685-3

Illustrations by Suzanne Langelier-Hamill

First edition
B C D E

To my daughter Casey,
with hopes that men in her future
will know how to build
effective human relationships

Acknowledgments

Many people have offered valuable help during the preparation of this book, and it would be impossible to remember them all adequately here. My students have been especially important in bringing up essential points, and as always my clients are a continual source of learning for me as we work together. My wife, Betsy, has again been my toughest editor, reading all of the rough drafts of chapters and offering her insights and encouragement. Lorna Brown helped immeasurably at all stages of the writing, providing moral support along the way. Finally, my editor at Harcourt Brace Jovanovich, Peggy Brooks, has done a remarkable job in clarifying the focus of the book, and I thank her for her careful work on the manuscript.

Contents

Good Sex

Introduction

Sex therapy is a relatively new field. For years there weren't any reliable approaches that had been tested on large numbers of men and women and that could be counted on to yield predictably good results. Then the early 1970s brought the sex therapy revolution. Masters and Johnson published their book, *Human Sexual Inadequacy*, describing for professionals a variety of techniques that they had tested for the treatment of several common functional problems in sex. That was just a beginning, and sex therapy has been growing ever since.

I had been involved in sex education and counseling for several years, and professional acquaintances frequently referred to me people with sexual complaints. When someone would come to my office concerned about lack of orgasm, or ejaculating too rapidly, or not being able to get turned on, I often found myself floundering. That's when I began to work toward getting the necessary background and certification to be a sex therapist. The more I work with people in sex therapy, the more I've been able to determine the most successful techniques.

My clientele in counseling and therapy is predominantly male, partly because I work at a college that has a high proportion of men in the student body and faculty and probably partly because I am a man. It is usually harder for men than it is for women to admit they have a problem and get started working on it, but once they get started, the treatment will usually be a success.

There is a sense of mystery about sex therapy that is undeserved. Medicine and the other helping professions create a kind of complicated aura around things that often are quite simple. As this book shows, the principles of sex therapy are built on common sense and good communication—not very mysterious at all.

The common sense aspect first became very clear to me when I experienced a sexual problem myself. It was a new relationship, and I was too embarrassed to talk with my partner about my sexual difficulty. Our relationship was full of guilts and worries. As I look back on this situation, I realize how ridiculously simple my "cure" turned out to be. I was discussing things with a counselor friend of mine, and he concluded by saying, "With all this crap going on in your life, it's not surprising it's showing up in sex." That was all I needed— permission to feel what I needed to feel, along with the realization that I wasn't reacting any differently from the way any man would in my situation. That helped me to feel that I could talk the problem over with my partner, who was also very understanding. The problem disappeared almost immediately and never returned. Of course, sex therapy isn't always that simple, but it need not be terribly complicated.

I also believe strongly that sex therapy should not be prohibitively expensive for anyone and that individual men and women are capable of knowing how long they should spend with each stage of treatment. Another myth common in sex therapy is that the only way to work on sexual problems is with your spouse or sexual partner. I found that many men without partners for therapy can make good progress alone on improving their sexual functioning, eventually bringing their success to partnership sex. The exercises in *Good Sex* emphasize self-help approaches, as well as techniques that you may use with a cooperative partner. Many of the exercises appear in this book for the first time, although each of them has been used successfully with my male clients. They can work for you also.

1

Men and Good Sex

This book is for males who want to work for more total sexual fulfillment through a greater awareness of their bodies, emotions, and abilities to communicate with other human beings. The sexually fulfilled man doesn't have to be a successful business wizard, football player, or conqueror of women by the score. Nor does he have to look like a movie star or a weight lifter. But he has learned to listen to his body and his feelings and has found there an increased pleasure in sex. He can communicate with those he cares about and can face difficulties—sexual and otherwise—when they occur.

The chapters ahead do not deal just with sexual problems. Rather, the approach of this book is to show you how improving your sex life is a matter of a greater awareness and understanding of your relationships with sexual partners and the messages and pleasurable feelings that your body has to offer you.

The healthy man never stops changing and growing. He feels good enough about himself, and has his life in clear enough perspective, that sex is not everything to him but is a happy, enjoyable part of his total being. He does not expect just to serve sexually, or to be served, but instead wants to share the pleasures of sex.

As a sex therapist, I am usually consulted by people who want primarily to improve their sexual functioning. Men worry about too little or too much interest in sex, not being able to keep an erection, ejaculating too soon during their sexual encounters, or not being able to reach orgasm at all. Arnie, for example, came in for his first session complaining of erection problems. Several of his recent attempts to have sex had ended abruptly when his penis had failed to cooperate.

Arnie put it this way: "I just want to be able to get it up and keep it up, or I might as well give up on being a man." Helping him to get his penis back into action would be simple enough, but getting him to realize that his sexual performance was only part of being a fulfilled and adequate man was harder.

Sex has become the target at which many modern males aim their manhood, and the battleground where partnership conflicts are fought. Some men think of sex as a carefully engineered performance and believe that it is their responsibility to see that it is done with technical precision. Others equate sex with conquest and the need to confirm their male identity. Add to that some men's feeling that they must be in control of every situation, and it is easy to see why technical efficiency in sex holds such importance for them.

Lee was a client of mine who was having so much difficulty in bed he was almost ready to abandon his sex life altogether. In one of our early sessions together, I tried to find out if he enjoyed touching his body and having his sexual partners touch him. About the only part of his body he touched very often, or liked to have touched during sex, was his penis. As he put it, "That's where all the action is." It was a sure sign to me that Lee was cut off from the totality of the rest of his body and his sexuality.

For a long time now, many men have ignored the pleasure that comes from experiencing sex with the whole body. They also tend to cut themselves off from their full range of emotions, not realizing that feelings are a vital part of sex.

Straighten up and act like a man

The narrow, got-to-do-it-right attitude toward sex is only one of the ways males end up getting cheated out of realizing their full potential as men. Recently I saw a man clip his young son briskly on the shoulder and say, "Straighten up and act like a man!" I felt myself redden with anger, although I was not about to say anything to another parent about his child-rearing tactics. Later, I was trying to figure out why the man's remark to his son had angered me. I realized that deep within my own being was a well of resentment about having been told the same sort of thing. I also realized that two of the words particularly struck raw nerves: *straighten* and *act*. They really are what much of manhood has been about for a long time: being straight as an arrow and acting.

Straight. What better word could be used to capture the ideal of American maleness. A *straight* penis ready to function sexually on demand. A *straight* face betraying only those feelings that may be shown at a specified time. A *straight* backbone and *straight* shoulders and legs that can stand up to any load or pressure and run *straight* down the playing field. *Straight* logic that enables us to shoot our decisions, clearly and concisely, *straight* from the hip. A *straight* sex life that prohibits sexual or sensual attachment to anything or anyone except a woman, particularly between her legs. These constitute what "straightening up" is all about.

Through years of practice, men learn the straight manhood script well. The American male knows how to make "manly" pursuits the center of his life and how to monitor his emotions with care. He can "read" others and then decide how much of himself to commit in return. The script makes him logical, adept at understanding the character of others, firm but fair-thinking, and a selfless friend, always willing to lend a hand. Yet under it all exists a real but partial human being cut off from much of his human potential.

Many males sell themselves to their jobs and gradually pull away from other parts of their lives, including sex. John, a thirty-five-year-old factory manager with three children, is a good example of such a man. John drags home nearly every evening too tired to do much of anything but have two drinks, eat his dinner, watch television, and fall asleep in his chair. Two or three nights a week he has job-related meetings or meetings with community groups to which he belongs. Except for taking the family on a two-week camping trip every year, inviting his wife to two conventions a year and out to dinner a couple of times every month, and initiating sex with her once or twice per week, he has given up all aspects of life that do not have something to do with his job. John is chronically fatigued, often irritable, usually feels pressured, and seldom is *really* happy. But he carries with him a vague knowledge that he is making it in the business world and a sense that at some point in the future he'll just be able to relax and enjoy himself. Most people regard him as a real mover with a future in the company, the best of providers, and a model citizen for his grateful community.

His wife, Helen, and the three kids see him that way too. Early in the marriage Helen went through many months of feeling neglected and ignored but eventually found her own interests and ways of coping with what she viewed as a fairly standard married life. She set aside her own sexual needs. The kids used to complain that their father didn't spend enough time with them, but they've adjusted now too. In a sense, John has been written off as little more than a breadwinner whose job requires a great personal sacrifice of time and energy. Much of the rest of him—including his interest in sex—has been lost.

Manhood scripts can be lethal

Martin grew up learning his male role well. In high school he was a football star. He advanced to officer status in the marines and later became a successful businessman. He was everyone's ideal of what a "real" man should be. After four years as a vice-president of his company, at the age of thirty-eight, he suffered a serious heart attack. As part of some work I was doing in the hospital at that time, I stopped in to see

Martin about a week after the attack. He was doodling on a yellow pad and looking very depressed. "I feel like I should be doing some work," he said with a weak smile, "but I haven't got the heart for it right now." As we continued talking, he cried some. He knew what had happened to him. "I drove myself until this happened. Always playing the game, trying to get ahead. Always pushing. Now that it's too late, I can see that it was never what I really wanted at all." He also worried that his sex life was now finished.

As things turned out, after Martin recovered from his coronary, he courageously took a big step away from the driving businessman role that he realized had never really fit him. He resigned from his company and moved with his wife and three children to a small resort village in the Thousand Islands. He travels occasionally as a consultant for some large industries but most of his time is spent as a self-employed real estate agent. When I visited him seven years after his heart attack, I found a relaxed, happy man who told me, "I don't have to prove anything to anybody. I set my own working hours now, and June [his wife] works right along with me. We spend plenty of time with each other and with the kids. No more of that phony competitive rat race to prove what a great man I am. To me, being a man means being happy and satisfied with myself. And sex has never been better."

Martin's old male role just didn't agree with him and in fact nearly killed him. That doesn't mean these roles aren't right for anyone else. Some men really enjoy being competitive and aggressive. But others don't care so much about getting ahead in their careers and prefer to relax, love, and be with their children.

Choice and good sex
It's up to you to accept responsibility for whatever shape your life happens to be in, sexually and in every other way. Your life reflects your choices. Certainly there are outside pressures and other people's needs to be considered. But you can't ever lose track of your own needs as well.

The sexually fulfilled man is responsible for choices in his sexual life also. Whether he generally feels satisfied with his own body and sexual activities, rather than frustrated, dried up, and unfulfilled, depends on several levels of these choices.

Level 1: your own body. The strength of any sexual partnership is rooted in the way each individual feels about himself or herself. One of my male clients saw himself as a skinny, out-of-proportion, undeveloped runt. The few times he had attempted sex with a partner, he had found it impossible to keep his erection. He used several of the body exploration exercises in this book, as well as a shape-up program, to give himself a more positive attitude toward his own body, and before long he developed more confidence in his appearance and physical "normalcy." Naturally his sex life improved. You can choose to like or dislike your own body and decide to change many of the things you dislike. You can also become more comfortable with your sex organs and all other parts of your sexuality.

Level 2: what kind of sex. Good sex requires that you decide what kinds of sexual activities are the biggest turn-ons for you and what sorts of partners you desire. Many men let society tell them what they should enjoy, never really taking a close look at their own sexual individuality.

A group of men in their middle and late twenties eventually got around to discussing masturbation. Taylor listened carefully for a long time before he took a deep breath and said, "I'm really surprised at how good the rest of you guys feel about masturbating. I've always thought I was doing something wrong that I should have stopped when I was fifteen. I've tried to do it as little as possible and try to screw every chick in sight to get rid of my sexual tension. I don't want to give up screwing, but I sure would like to be able to relax and let myself enjoy masturbation when I want to. I just never realized I might be able to see it as okay." Taylor is a good example of a man who had lost faith in himself and the sexual things he enjoyed.

Level 3: when to have sex. Jeremy knew what turned him on sexually but he hadn't bothered to question his choice of the best times to have sex. He took a different partner to his apartment several nights a week and thought he was living an ideal playboy's sex life. Still he was bored and dissatisfied and he didn't know why. As he and I talked about sex, it became clear that his goal for every evening out was only scoring, yet he actually wanted more out of sex than that. He began to think about when sex was best for him and his partners and then to make some real choices about his sex life.

Level 4: the whys of sex. Perhaps the most complicated sexual questions involve the whys of sex. Some men insist that you should just do it and not worry about the reasons why, but sex is too important to take for granted. I know one couple for whom sex had become mechanical and boring. They did some of the mutual body-pleasuring exercises in this book, and then I asked them to consider why they were having sex at all. A week later, one of them put it this way: "That's been our problem—doing it without any particularly good reason. It feels good, but we want it to be more than that. Then we started talking about it and decided that both of us think sex is a great thing to share. It can make us feel really close and warm together—almost like we're fused together. Other times it can just be for kicks too. And we can do other things with sex, like apologize or give something nice to one another. But we've decided to stop having sex just because it's the night we usually have it."

HOW GOOD SEX CAN BE

Most people who come into my office for help with sexual problems think of sex as something you *do* rather than something you *are*. Your sexuality is not just your genitals and sex acts; it permeates your life and personality. It includes your body and how you feel about it, your emotions and how they are expressed, your attitudes and values, and the roles you have learned to act out as a man.

The people who attract you sexually, and what you enjoy doing sexually, are parts of your *sexual individuality*. Everybody has his or her own set of sexually interesting activities and turn-ons, as individualized as fingerprints. Most people spend more time worrying about their sexual specialties than they do enjoying them. By the time you reach the end of this book, you should feel more comfortable with your sexual preferences and have a clearer idea of what you want out of sex.

There are men who could care less about sex with women, and women who are not interested in sex with men. There are people who enjoy other forms of sex more than intercourse. There are those who want to have intercourse with members of the opposite sex sometimes but would rather do other things with other partners at other times. Also, it's important to understand that your sexual needs and preferences are not built into you like concrete. Some parts of your sexuality remain stable throughout your life; some parts change or go through temporary phases. The more open you are to the possibilities of change, the more apt you are to change.

Some people feel that sex should be done only for *procreation*—to make babies. But most have sex for other reasons. Sex can be great *recreation* too, and here I am referring to the entire broad spectrum of sexual activities, not just intercourse. It can be fun, it can feel good, and it can renew the spirit. Sex can also be a *celebration of love*, as two people become more and more intimate and share their bodies' pleasures. In loving relationships, sex can be a special form of communication.

There are loads of other reasons. Sometimes a man uses sex to relieve anxiety or restlessness, sometimes to build up feelings of self-confidence in his masculinity. Other times he uses it to express anger or hatred or sympathy. For most people, sex is somewhat addictive. You keep coming back for more.

This book isn't going to try to explain why people want a

particular form of sex. Most of the time that probably doesn't even matter. For you, the important thing is that you (and your partner, if you have one) feel happy and contented with the type of sexual activity you've chosen.

Breaking out of old molds

A friend of mine recently told me about his experience in an awareness group on the West Coast. The group had consisted of men and women who met several times, primarily to talk but also to experiment with some touching exercises together. A lot of people think that "touchy-feely" stuff is silly, strange, or just a sly way to get some sexual kicks, and for some, it is. But others have discovered that such exercises help them to learn more about themselves and their attitudes toward relationships. Anyway, while blindfolded, my friend Pete was paired up with another person, and the two were told to explore each other's hands (only) without talking at all. Pete said that immediately he knew that he had been paired with a woman. The skin was soft, the fingers gentle and caressing. The two intertwined their fingers and explored one another carefully, almost lovingly. Pete said he could feel himself responding with sexual arousal and noticed his penis hardening.

After a few minutes, all were told to remove their blindfolds. Pete was surprised and embarrassed to discover he had been fondling the hands of another *man*. He told me that his first reaction was to think, *goddamn pansy*. The other man looked equally perplexed as the group leader told each one to discuss his reactions. As Pete and the other man talked over what had happened, it became clear that each had thought he had been paired with a woman. Neither of them had hairy hands, nor skin toughened from manual labor. Since both had assumed the other was female, both had made a special effort to be gentle and loving. Both reported being attracted sexually only to women and felt a little scared by their experience. As Pete told me: "It was then I realized how silly my negative attitude toward homosexuals was, and how cut off from other males I really am. If that hand had been attached to a vagina,

I would have been able to love it and make love to it. At this point in my life, I wouldn't want to have sex with another guy, but I can understand how some men would be turned on by that. More importantly, though, I *do* want to be able to touch another guy and enjoy it, without getting all hung up about what's wrong with me sexually. I guess since I was young, I have been learning my lesson well. Now I'm too scared and guilty to be anything but heterosexual."

Many people think homosexuals are sick individuals who may be a danger to our society. I have found a number of men who are shocked when they discover sexual interests in themselves that they consider unusual, abnormal, or "perverted." Their fears are rooted in sexual standards established about one hundred years ago, which today are changing. Traditionally, the only "permissible" sex was penis-in-the-vagina intercourse that might produce offspring and that happened only between married couples. Nobody, particularly a woman, was supposed to linger very much with the whole operation or enjoy it very much. Other forms of sexual behavior got branded as "perverse." Masturbation was thought to lead to a variety of serious diseases in the body and mind.

Men and women are breaking out of their old sexual molds. Many—probably most—psychiatrists, psychologists, and counselors no longer automatically view homosexuality, masturbation, or other forms of sex as signs of problems. In fact, a very prevalent view among professionals today is that any kind of sexual need or activity that a person finds satisfying and enjoyable is perfectly all right, providing it doesn't hurt or take advantage of a partner. Also, most people are beginning to realize that almost everyone can enjoy many forms of sexual activity, depending on the situation and the other person(s) involved.

Having the freedom to break out of old molds has its dangers. You could try too much too soon. As you find yourself moving in new directions sexually, remember to rely on your inner feelings to let you know what seems right for your life and relationships.

Who seduces and satisfies whom?

Seduction has become a dirty word, implying that a man or woman is lured into a sexual encounter with false promises. Traditionally, the male has been seen as the seducer whose goal of scoring is more than obvious. Some think of the female as a crafty seductress who entices partners to her bed with sly, seemingly innocent games. Fortunately, contemporary men and women have put aside these old stereotypes and participate in mutual seduction, not a dirty term at all. Good sex always has an element of seduction to it, and the best form is when each of you enjoys seducing the other, fully understanding what you are looking for.

Couples who have healthy, growing sexual relationships often enjoy being seductive to one another. I was talking with a male friend about a book that recommends all sorts of gimmicks women can use to turn men on. He laughed about having given the book to his wife as a joke. He also added, "She knows I have a thing for panties and garters. So the night after I gave her the book, she met me at the door in these silky bikini panties and a garter belt. We had a good laugh, but some really good sex too. She gets turned on by seeing bare-chested men in low-slung jeans. So the next night I paraded around the living room with no shirt and with the fly of my jeans half unzipped. It was another great night."

The important thing about this couple's sex life was that they recognized each other's desires and took turns playing the seducer, instead of one having always to be the leader. In addition, they didn't really take themselves too seriously. They knew that sexy games are fun once in a while but would get boring eventually. The man also recognized something that many men simply don't realize: women have particular sexual tastes in partners too. Women have their own quirks and kinks and special things that turn them on.

If you expect your partner to meet your every need and always to be sexually available, you are also missing out on the fun of sharing and growing together sexually. Both partners in a sexual relationship must take responsibility for their own sexual satisfaction, while being responsive and sensitive *to each other*. Either one should have the right *not* to be sexy sometimes and to decline sexual activity. Men are not always more interested in sex than women, nor are they always ready for action. In many couples, in fact, it is the woman who has stronger sexual desires than the man. And very few people want or need sex all the time.

Good sex

As I work with men on expanding their sexual enjoyment and reaching toward sexually fulfilled manhood, I realize that much of what we accomplish could have been done without a face-to-face visit with me or any therapist. Although sex counselors and therapists are necessary for many people (Chapter 7 includes suggestions for when and how to find professional help), a book with exercises such as this can help a lot of men. There are also many males who want to improve their sex lives but choose not to seek out a professional therapist, are not close enough to such a person to make convenient visits, or simply cannot afford such help.

New views of men and women are having a direct effect on some men's sex lives too. Many women feel freed to get more in touch with their sexual feelings and to want more out of sex themselves. This can mean new experiences and sexual opportunities for their male partners. Some men are uncomfortable with this, but others are turned on.

The major part of this book concentrates on the technical improvement of sex. Not only may that be important to your feelings about yourself, but it makes sex more enjoyable for everyone. However, to work on bettering erections and orgasms without working on understanding all the aspects of maleness would be a disservice to everyone who reads this book. Being male is more than having an active penis.

Within every human being there is a special dynamic quality, the tremendous capacity to *change*. The exercises in the pages ahead can be catalysts for becoming involved in a process of change, a process of working toward being a more fully functioning, satisfied, dynamic, and flexible man—sexually as well as in many other ways.

This is a *self-help book*, requiring that you take responsibility for yourself. The book will work with your own sense of responsibility and motivation to help you begin a process of change. The suggested exercises are flexible and may be selected and used in very individualized ways.

Your own wide world of sex: a questionnaire

Before continuing to read this book and do the exercises suggested in its various chapters, it would be a good idea for you to take a closer look at your own sex life, past and present. The following questions may help you think a little more about the sexual things you have done and the ones you have most enjoyed. If you would prefer not writing your answers in the book, use a separate sheet of paper or simply think about the answers. You may also want to have your sexual partner complete the questionnaire, so that you can talk over your answers together.

1. Do you remember the first time you saw an adult in the nude? ———— Yes ———— No
   If so, did you get at all sexually aroused by seeing this person? ———— Yes ———— No ———— Don't remember

2. What do you remember as the first sexual experience you ever had with another person? ————————————
   How do you feel about this experience as you look back on it now? ————————————

3. What was the first sexually oriented "dirty" word you remember learning? ———————— Do you ever use the word now? ———— Yes ———— No

4. Under what circumstances do you usually get excited sexually?

_____ Hardly ever   _____ Necking or petting
_____ Looking at sexy   _____ During foreplay
       pictures   _____ Other (explain):
_____ Dancing   _____
_____ Thinking or fanta-
       sizing about sex

5. At what age can you remember having your first or-
   gasm? _____
   (Males only) Have you ever experienced a nocturnal
   emission, or "wet dream"? _____ Yes _____ No
   If so, how frequently do you experience them now?
   _____ Never _____ Very rarely _____ Occasionally
   _____ Once a month _____ Weekly or more frequently

6. Have you ever had a spontaneous orgasm while awake,
   without deliberately handling your sex organs?
   _____ Yes _____ No
   If so, under what circumstances?
   _____ Looking at a picture _____ Thinking about sex
   _____ Necking or petting _____ Dancing
   _____ Other (explain): _____

7. At approximately what age did you begin masturbating? _____
   How frequently do you masturbate now?
   _____ 10 or more times weekly _____ Daily
   _____ 3–5 times weekly _____ 1–2 times weekly
   _____ 2–3 times monthly _____ Once a month
   _____ Less than monthly _____ Never
   How did you first learn to masturbate? _____

8. Have you ever been approached by a friend or stranger
   of your same sex who wanted to have a sexual experience
   with you? _____ Yes _____ No
   Did you have some form of sexual contact with someone
   of your same sex when you were 15 years old or younger?
   _____ Yes _____ No
   If so, what did your contact(s) include?

_____ Examining or meas-
uring sex organs
_____ Masturbating each
other
_____ Mouth-genital con-
tacts
_____ Anal intercourse or
contact

_____ Masturbating at
the same time
_____ Kissing and
touching
_____ Experimenting
with intercourse
positions
_____ Other (explain):

_____

Have you had sexual contact(s) with someone of your
same sex since the age of 15? _____ Yes _____ No
If so, did you reach orgasm during these contacts?
_____ Yes _____ No
With how many different same-sexed partners have you
participated in sex? _____

9. Did you have some form of sexual contact with someone
of the opposite sex when you were 15 years old or
younger? _____ Yes _____ No
If so, what did your contact(s) include?
_____ Looking at each
other's sex organs
_____ Experimenting
with intercourse
positions
_____ Sexual intercourse

_____ Feeling each
other's sex organs
_____ Mouth-genital
contact
_____ Other (explain):

_____

10. Check as many of the following experiences as you have
had with another person since the age of 15:
_____ Being completely nude together
_____ Having our sex organs in contact while clothed
_____ Having our sex organs in contact while nude
_____ Having mouth contact with the other's sex organs
_____ Other person having mouth contact with your sex
organs
_____ Having simultaneous mouth–sex organ contact
(69)

_____ Sexual contact for which the other person paid you

11. Have you had sexual intercourse with someone of the opposite sex since the age of 15?
_____ Yes _____ No
If so, answer the following questions:
With how many different partners have you had intercourse? _____
In the past six months, how often—on the average—have you experienced sexual intercourse?
_____ Never _____ Several times, but only during an isolated period
_____ Less than once per month _____ Once per month
_____ Twice per month _____ Once per week
_____ 2–3 times per week _____ 4–7 times per week
_____ 8 or more times per week
In the past six months, how often have you reached orgasm during intercourse?
_____ Every time _____ Every time except once
_____ Almost every time _____ About 75% of the time
_____ About 50% of the time _____ About 25% of the time
_____ Once or twice _____ A few times
_____ Never
On the average, how much time is required for you to reach orgasm . . . During intercourse: _____ minutes
During masturbation: _____ minutes

12. During a single sexual contact, typically how many times do you reach orgasm? _____

13. Have you ever shared a sex experience with more than one other person at a time? _____ Yes _____ No
Have you ever participated in sexual activity with another person while other people were having sex in the same room? _____ Yes _____ No

14. Check any of the following that have been of real concern

to you during your lifetime and indicate whether they
were of concern during adolescence and/or since adolescence:

During Adolescence	Since Adolescence	
――	――	Size or shape of your sex organs
――	――	Size or shape of your breasts
――	――	General physical appearance
――	――	Masturbation
――	――	Homosexual arousal or attraction
――	――	Homosexual activity
――	――	Pregnancy or fear of pregnancy in partner
――	――	Abortion
――	――	Venereal disease
――	――	Extramarital sexual activity (in self, partner, or parents)
――	――	Inability to achieve orgasm
――	――	Ejaculating too soon
――	――	Impotence (difficulty with erection)
――	――	Painful intercourse (for you or partner)
――	――	Loss of virginity
――	――	Too much sexual desire
――	――	Too little sexual desire
――	――	Fear of the opposite sex
――	――	Sexual fantasies
――	――	Failure to "please" a sexual partner
――	――	Lack of cooperation in sex from a partner
――	――	Sexual interests or activities you consider "unusual"
――	――	Other (explain): ――――

15. Have you ever . . .

Had sex with a child or minor during your adult life? _____ Yes _____ No

Had sexual contact with an animal? _____ Yes _____ No

Enjoyed showing your sex organs to another person? _____ Yes _____ No

Peeked in a window or door, trying to see someone in the nude or sexually involved? _____ Yes _____ No

Participated in sex where pain, bondage, or domination was used for arousal? _____ Yes _____ No

Been turned on by dressing up in clothing of the opposite sex? _____ Yes _____ No

After completing the questionnaire, think for a few minutes about how you answered various questions. Were there any questions you hesitated to answer? If so, why? Do you feel uncomfortable about any of your answers or believe yourself to be "unusual" because of any of them? Did you give any false answers? You can be sure that whatever you have done sexually, there are plenty of others who have done the same things. How *you feel* about your sexual activities is most important. If you are uncomfortable with some aspects of your sexuality or find that you are not functioning the way you would like to be, then this book can probably help. Even if you're relatively satisfied, this book may give you some suggestions to improve your sex life even more. Read on.

2

Your Most Potent Sex Organ: Communication

I had first met Nick at a social gathering. He was sitting off in a corner by himself, and I sought him out because he looked as uncomfortable as I felt. I am not much good at cocktail hour small talk. He seemed fascinated by my profession and asked several questions about counseling and therapy. He eventually got around to asking if he might have an appointment with me sometime, so I explained the procedure to him and gave him the telephone number.

By the time I saw Nick in my office three weeks later, he was ready to pour out his story. He was a twenty-five-year-old unmarried teacher, a little on the short side but good-looking. "I just don't understand why I can't make it with women," he moaned. "No matter what I try, it doesn't seem to be the right approach. I'm shy, but I force myself to get out whenever possible, and I make myself talk to women, even though I get really nervous. I try to be casual, you know, and talk about any subject that comes up. I keep informed on a lot of things, and I know about sailing and skiing. But no matter what I talk about, women seem to drift away eventually to talk to somebody else."

Nick felt especially inadequate about sex. His most painful revelation to me was that he was still a virgin. "I am probably the only twenty-five-year-old straight guy in this state who hasn't had intercourse," he said. "I've done other things with women, but when it gets right down to the wire, I just don't know how to get them into bed for the real thing. Later I feel really inadequate and immature." He had seemingly tried everything. He had read books, gotten suggestions from friends who were "making it," and rehearsed for hours in front of the mirror, but something just was not clicking for him.

Communication impotence

Nick was suffering from what I call *communication impotence*. His way of dealing with women was superficial, and he was all tied up with phony ideas on the male "image" and myths about the way men *should* communicate. His difficulties really boiled down to one main problem: he never relaxed and tried to be *himself*. Following are some manhood myths that got in the way of Nick's ability to communicate. They are very common among males and often prevent good and lasting relationships. See how many of these myths you believe and have used:

Myth 1: men should always be confident. Shyness and uncertainty have not been respected male qualities during communication. A strong, unwavering voice and direct approach are the way "real men" are supposed to talk. Yet, how inhuman all that is and how much practice it takes to look that way. Take a close look at some conversations the next time you are in a bar or at a party or business gathering, and see the signs of tension and bluffing. The fact of the matter is, most people feel shy and uncomfortable in new situations or while talking with strangers. And why shouldn't they? New situations are a little scary and sometimes make people feel insecure. There is that initial tense period when you are face-to-face with a new person and begin evaluating what you have to offer each other. If you feel confident, secure, and comfortable in these settings, fine. But if you feel a little shy and insecure, that's okay too. You can be sure that plenty of other people feel the same way.

Myth 2: men have all the answers. I overheard a conversation in a restaurant recently in which a woman and a man were discussing whether or not men were turned off by women who came up to them and asked them to dance. "Men don't like aggressive chicks," this man told his female companion. "It's just not feminine to do the asking." A mild argument followed between the two, but he stood his ground. Not only was this guy locked into some rigid sex roles and scripts, but he had set himself up as the spokesman for "real men" everywhere. That is common in male communication. Men often seem to feel they must have an opinion on every issue and an answer to every question. Many times I have seen men who really don't have much of an opinion or any solid information make something up on the spot—just because they are afraid of looking foolish. Saying, "I don't know much about that" doesn't appeal to men who live by the myth that they should have all the answers.

Myth 3: an impressive conversationalist never permits any dead air. The most frightening part of any conversation is silence. You begin to fidget. Your eyes search around trying to avoid the other person's gaze. You shift your weight to the other foot. You hunt in your mind for something to say but momentarily cannot find any fresh topics. The manhood script by which most men live demands that there be very little silence. It says that they should try to know something about everything so that they will be able to hold up their end of any conversation. Maybe that's why so many people look bored or preoccupied when they are conversing. Why is silence so frightening? For many people, it's because words are a way of holding others away, keeping them at "word's length." So when the words fail, the silence forces a new kind of intimacy. The two of you have to look at each other a little more and search together for more words to fill the air. But momentarily there is a sense of intimacy—of just simply, quietly sharing each other—that most men don't like. Yet being able to shut up sometimes, and especially to listen, may be among the most essential elements for really getting to know another person and letting him or her get to know you.

Myth 4: mapping out strategies ahead of time makes for better communication. Nick told me about the advice one of his friends had given him before going to a party. He had been told: "Stay loose. Keep three or four things in mind to talk about, but only use them when the conversation lags. Don't look too interested. Smile a lot to yourself and look a little bored. When you look hard to get, women chase even harder. When you're ready to get things really moving, tell her you're sick of the party and she's welcome to join you at your apartment if she wants. But don't look too anxious." Nick tried it all and felt like a fool. He probably looked like one too. Planned strategies just set up games to which only one person knows the rules. Sometimes they work, but then you have established a relationship on a dishonest ground that will eventually give way. Being yourself is almost always the best "strategy."

Myth 5: men should know how to talk about "manly" things. Many men feel obligated to be able to discuss sports, business, politics, war, and other traditionally "manly" pursuits. What they sometimes forget is that the person to whom they are talking may not have any interest in these topics. Some people play the game of "Let him talk about himself and his interests, and he'll feel so good I can get what I want." Next time you are at a place where people gather socially, look around at some of the male-female conversations you see going on. You'll probably see a few women hanging on every word that the men are using. You'll also see women who look bored stiff and obviously wish their dates would shut up. And listen to men ramble on about teams and scores and production and candidates and Vietnam experiences and a variety of other manly subjects guaranteed eventually to bore even the most dedicated conversationalist. There is always a place for such topics, but lots of men simply don't have any interest in some of these areas, even though they feel obligated to take part in the conversation. Good communication also must leave a place for personal sharing as well—of feelings, dreams, hopes; and discomforts. We need inside topics as well as "out there" ideas.

Myth 6: a real man can use the right line to convince a partner to have sex. I have heard men discussing the "lines" that have proved most effective for them in persuading partners to go to bed. I have also heard women practicing effective answers to these propositions. Some men measure their masculinity by the number of their sexual conquests.

Those are some of the myths that represent a surefire prescription for stifling communication. Most of them are rooted in the manhood script and are guaranteed to stimulate the development of games, phony conversation, and shallow relationships. A sexual relationship that grows out of this kind of communication probably doesn't have much hope in the long run. And when communication is lacking, little sexual problems are very likely to turn into big ones.

Men and their emotional dams

Few men are able to express their most intense feelings outwardly. Instead, they dam them up, perhaps not realizing how dangerous dammed-up feelings may become. An emotion kept inside can create tension or other chemical changes in the body. So without realizing what they are doing, many men turn their fears into headaches and backaches, their anger at not getting ahead into ulcers, their frustration into high blood pressure, and their anxiety and depression into sexual problems. It is seldom that men permit themselves to feel and express a whole and real emotion—unedited and uncensored.

Some men learn from their fathers to be as uncommunicative as possible about emotions and other personal aspects of their lives. These same men often believe the myth of the nagging woman. They see women as always being "at men," trying to pry into their thoughts and feelings. Actually, many women get so frustrated by men that they do become bitchy and nag at them. Margo and Jed showed this typical pattern. As Jed put it, "Women are always talking or crying. I figure the less said, the better. I can handle my own problems and don't need any help from anybody. She gets upset all the time, and I try not to pay any attention to her. Otherwise, she'll start taking herself seriously."

Margo had about reached the end of her rope. "Most of the time he acts like I don't even exist," she complained. "He is so strong all of the time. He never lets anything show on the outside. I feel like I live with a rock instead of a human being. I want so much to get to know him better, to find out what he's really like inside. He acts as if I don't count at all and that my feelings are silly and unnecessary. I get so frustrated that I end up getting mad, and I nag at him. Then I feel rotten about that." In male-female partnerships, for every nagging woman there is usually a dammed-up man who finds it difficult to be a real human being with feelings. For every sexual problem, there are usually one or two people who have trouble communicating thoughts and feelings to each other.

Men are hesitant to express emotions, partly in order to protect themselves. They are competitive and want to come out on top, looking better than the next person. Naturally, it follows that they fear being vulnerable and associate expression of emotion with vulnerability.

As an example, Sam was telling me one day about an angry encounter he had the night before with his girl friend. They had been having continuing difficulties in their relationship, and this was a typical example of their trouble in dealing openly with feelings. Jennie had come into the bathroom while Sam was shaving and had remarked that he seemed to be getting quite bald. Sam's face reddened with anger as he told me about it. "I told her that she didn't seem to be getting any younger herself," he recalled, "and that her breasts were already sagging. That showed her. Then we started arguing about the same old other crap all over again."

I knew that Sam took great pride in his appearance and tried to keep himself in good shape. I suggested that he retrace his steps back to the angry incident the night before and try to remember what he was feeling underneath all of his anger.

As he thought about it and we talked some more, the anger went out of his voice. "It's important to me that Jennie find me attractive. When she made that crack, she hit something deep inside, and I felt hurt and depressed."

"So why did you only show anger on the outside?" I asked.

"Oh, I don't know. I guess partly because it would have seemed silly to get so upset about a simple remark like that. But also, if I told Jennie how much she had bothered me, it would be like giving her the upper hand. You know, then she'll know exactly how to get to me."

Sam had trapped himself into a pattern with Jennie that was bound to build into more trouble. His anger had been a phony cover-up. He had dammed up his real feelings of hurt and disappointment. His manhood script would not permit him to show the hurt, maybe even cry a little, even though he probably felt like it inside. I tried to get him to see how much better the situation could have been if he had trusted Jennie enough to let her know what he was really feeling. She probably had no idea how much her remark had hurt him and would want to talk things out if she knew. If she didn't care enough to do that or enjoyed hurting him deliberately, then perhaps the relationship wasn't very stable or healthy anyway. But it would be better for both of them to face that fact instead of gradually tearing each other apart with superficial anger.

Sam had fallen into a common male trap. His competitiveness and fear of vulnerability, added to his lack of trust in other people, would not allow him to express his real feelings. So the emotions built tension in his body and showed anger when really there was a lot of hurt underneath.

When dammed-up emotions are brought into the bedroom, sex is heading for trouble. A good sexual relationship has to involve a letting go of feelings, an opening up and giving out. Sexual partners must be able to share their inner thoughts and feelings as well as their bodies. If they don't, their unexpressed emotions will generate tension, anxiety, fear, anger, or depression. Sex then begins to lose some of its satisfaction or perhaps fails completely.

TIME OUT

Parts of this chapter will help you examine and improve your own patterns of communication.

For men only

Try to remember the most recent experience you have had during which you felt tense and uncomfortable talking with another person in some social or business situation. Close your eyes and recall the incident in as much detail as possible. What were you talking about? Exactly what did you and the other person say? How did you act? How did you feel? Now take a closer look at that experience in view of the myths that lead to communication impotence. Rate yourself on the following statements, using this scale:

$$0 = \text{I was not doing/feeling this at all.}$$
$$1 = \text{I was doing/feeling this to a small extent.}$$
$$2 = \text{I was doing/feeling this about half the time.}$$
$$3 = \text{I was doing/feeling this most of the time.}$$
$$4 = \text{I was doing/feeling this all the time.}$$

Circle your rating: During the uncomfortable experience, as I recall it:

0	1	2	3	4	I was feeling nervous and shy, but trying to look confident and together.
0	1	2	3	4	I was trying hard to make my voice sound strong and stable.
0	1	2	3	4	My body felt tense and jittery.
0	1	2	3	4	I tried to look as if I knew what I was talking about, even when I didn't.

0	1	2	3	4	I wanted to look knowledgeable and intelligent.
0	1	2	3	4	I was uncomfortable each time there was a lag in the conversation.
0	1	2	3	4	I tried to talk whenever the other person was quiet.
0	1	2	3	4	I tried to anticipate the direction of the conversation ahead of time so that I could be ready.
0	1	2	3	4	I tried to project a certain image to the other person that wasn't really me.
0	1	2	3	4	We talked about sports, business, politics, the service, or other typically "manly" topics.
0	1	2	3	4	I talked about "manly" topics even when I wasn't interested in them.
0	1	2	3	4	I felt as if I had to compete with the other person in conversation and play "one-upmanship."
0	1	2	3	4	I was trying to think of the right things to say to persuade the other person to have sex with me.
0	1	2	3	4	I was trying to look and be sexy.
0	1	2	3	4	I felt unable to express some of my own real feelings.

When you have completed your ratings, add up the numbers and get a total score. If your score was 31 to 49, you may be getting yourself into a bind by paying a lot of attention to male communication myths. A score of 50 or over would indicate that at least during the experience you were recalling, you were constantly on guard, trying to live up to some of the traditional standards of masculine communication; if you want to improve your sex life, you may have to re-examine some of those ideas.

The next time you are communicating with someone, keep this rating scale in the back of your mind. Perhaps you can work toward keeping your score as low as possible, as an escape from your own manhood script.

Noticing feelings—an exercise for men

During your childhood and adolescence, what did you learn about expressing your feelings? For example, did you gradually learn that it was unacceptable for you to cry—at least around others? When you cried during late childhood, how did your parents react? What did they tell you? Did you learn not to look afraid, even when you were? Did you also learn that it was unmanly to giggle and laugh uncontrollably? Did you learn that to be gentle, caring, and loving was only for sissies? Those are some of the messages with which most young men grow up. Take a closer look at your emotional reactions by answering the following questions:

> When was the last time you cried in front of another person (or other people), and what were the circumstances that moved you to tears? Could you allow yourself to cry all you needed or did you try to stop yourself? Did you feel embarrassed? Do you consider the cause of your tears an acceptable or unacceptable reason for a man to cry? What makes it so?

> When was the last time you felt really angry toward another person? As you think back, try to look beneath your anger to find any other real feelings that were present. Were you actually hurt by something the other person had done or said? Did you feel as if you were losing something to the other person? How did you show your anger? Did you let it all out or store up most or all of it inside?

Here is a list of words describing some normal human feelings. For each emotion listed, indicate how much freedom you give yourself to *express* the feeling outwardly, so that it could be seen in your face or body. Use the following letters as a guide for rating each emotion, choosing the response that is *most* appropriate:

A = I feel comfortable expressing this feeling openly around any group of people.

B = I feel comfortable expressing this feeling with friends and trusted people.

C = I feel comfortable expressing this feeling only with my lover or very closest friend.

D = I do *not* feel comfortable expressing this feeling in front of any other person.

_____	Excitement	_____	Joy
_____	Frustration	_____	Loneliness
_____	Surprise	_____	Hatred
_____	Guilt	_____	Depression
_____	Love	_____	Sympathy
_____	Fear	_____	Boredom
_____	Happiness	_____	Pride
_____	Sadness	_____	Shame
_____	Hurt	_____	Anxiety
_____	Anger	_____	Disgust

Look back over the list of feelings, and particularly note the ones you have labeled with a *D*. What do you do with these feelings? Do you allow yourself to feel them in private, or does it seem as if you never actually feel them at all? Do you sometimes store them up inside? If so, do they generate tension or other discomfort?

DON'T LET YOUR PENIS
DO THE TALKING

When men come to me for help with sexual difficulties, I usually must spend time looking at the relationships they have and at the kinds of games they play. Lack of communication and stored-up feelings can eventually build roadblocks that prevent good sex. Many men find that their penises speak for them if they can't express themselves in words. When a man ejaculates before he wants to, or has difficulty getting an erection, or cannot seem to have an orgasm when he wants to, or simply doesn't get as much out of sex anymore, his penis may be doing all the talking. Here are some of the messages that penises give because the men behind them won't speak for themselves.

"Boy are you ugly"

There are loads of reasons why a man may be turned off by a sexual partner. He may think his partner unattractive with physical qualities that simply don't appeal to him. There may also be other things going on in the relationship that lead to rejection. It is difficult for a man to get sexually aroused by or fully enjoy sex with someone who disgusts or angers him. Yet many times a man figures he can still get his sexual kicks, regardless of his feelings toward the other person. It is not surprising that these sexual encounters often are flops.

"I don't feel sexy right now"

One of the biggest myths of human sexuality is the idea that men are constantly hungry for sex. Give a man an opportunity for an orgasm, and he'll grab it, right? Not necessarily. Men and women both have times when they are more interested in sex or feel sexier than at other times. Men also seem to go through unpredictable cycles of several weeks when they want a lot of sex and several weeks when they could care less most of the time. Those who try to "tough it out" in the face of negative emotions, only to find sex disappointing, begin to feel even *more* depressed, angry, guilty, or scared. In our busy world there are also the constant problems of *fatigue* and *being out of shape*. Like any other pleasurable body activity, sex works best and feels best when you are rested, relaxed, and in reasonably good physical condition. Those qualities will always go a long way toward improving sexual activity.

"I don't trust you"

Sharing sex with another person is a deeply intimate experience that is best when you open up and let go. You show someone else part of yourself others rarely see. When a man has an orgasm, his barriers are down. He's momentarily out of control and off guard. So, for sex to work well and be fully pleasurable between two people, there has to be some level of trust established between them. If a man doesn't trust his sexual partner to some degree, his penis will probably let him and the partner know eventually.

"Are you my mommy?"

Some men bring unresolved conflicts and emotional problems with them to their sexual relationships. One of my clients in sex therapy was a thirty-year-old man who had always had a stormy relationship with his mother. They had argued frequently and he often felt that he hated her. He had never quite resolved these feelings and instead generalized them against all women. His hidden negative feelings made him downright mean to his wife. He came to me because their sex life was in miserable shape. He rarely got an erection with her, and they had all but given up on intercourse. His unresolved problems with his mother surfaced before long, and he realized how many feelings he had been hiding inside. His penis knew all along, though, and had been doing all the talking for him.

"Who is supposed to be on top here?"

Sex is a common place for power games to be played out between two people. A man's fear of appearing vulnerable may be expressed in sexual positions. There are, for example, some men who cannot function sexually unless they are literally "on top of the situation." One of my clients could never have an orgasm while lying on his back, no matter what kind of stimulation his partner provided. Most power games are more subtle than that. One man I knew had a lot of dammed-up anger at his sexual partner, a woman who earned more money than he. He would always ejaculate long before she had a chance to enjoy intercourse at all. Counseling gradually revealed that this was his way of getting back at her, of "punishing" her for what he saw as her power in the financial success area. Rape is probably the ultimate male power play. Some men feel so negatively toward women and so inadequate themselves that they must force their penises on women to prove how "powerful" they are. Sex is rarely much good until neither partner has to worry about who is on top and power games are set aside.

"Just try and get me"

This is a variation on the power game theme. Lots of men and women know how to spoil sex by being unavailable at the "right" time. There is always the old headache standing by just in case, and it is used by men as well as women. Being drunk may also be a handy way either to avoid sex or to justify a sexual failure. Men make themselves unavailable by being too busy or too tired. They also make themselves hard to get by being emotionally unreachable and detached.

"But you said . . ."

Disappointment is a common problem in relationships, and the penis may express it by not functioning as desired. Many couples don't realize that the ground rules of their partnership may have to change with time. They enter into their relationship with all sorts of unwritten (and sometimes written) agreements, believing that things will always stay the same. They don't. And when one partner feels that the other is not living up to the agreement, disappointment, disillusionment, and anger may arise. If these concerns do not get worked out through effective communication, they will eventually show up in the sexual relationship. Sex cannot continue to be fully satisfying for long in a relationship where there is disappointment with each other or bitterness at having been cheated in some way.

"Could this be sabotage?"

In situations where communication is inadequate, sabotage is a handy weapon because you can escape a sexual encounter without looking like the guilty party. One of my clients was a man who had been troubled by impotence with his wife of seven years. He admitted to me during a therapy session one day that he always felt best after an argument with his mate, and that he was puzzled by this. It didn't take long to figure out that arguments generated enough anger so that his wife would not be interested in sex for a couple of days. So, for him the pressure was off—no need to worry about another sexual failure for a while. An easy way to sabotage sex is to drop some subtle criticisms about a partner's sexual performance. Nothing turns most people off more rapidly than worrying that they are being sexually inadequate in some way. It is also simple to make oneself unattractive so that a partner won't be interested anyway. People have chosen hair curlers, facial creams, cigar breath, underarm odor, unattractive clothes, too many pounds, and a variety of other means to sabotage sexual contacts. Some people try to frustrate their partner's sexual desires. One client enjoyed having his female partner move a great deal in sex. During a difficult period in their relationship, she would lie as still as possible, effectively sabotaging his sexual excitement. It is always amazing to me how much trouble people will go to in avoiding sex and in avoiding talking to each other. But as always, the penis will get the message across.

"Let's get this solved as soon as possible"

Probably most people play the game of "good communication." The main rule of the game is to get problems and bad feelings out of the way as quickly as possible. Actually, resolving difficulties between people takes time and work. However, in the "good communication" game, one person somehow decides what is really wrong and gives the other some quick advice on how to resolve the problem. Men are notorious as speedy problem solvers because they usually like to feel on top of every situation and don't like lingering over unpleasant emotions. So they jump in with their quick solutions. One of the standard approaches is to attempt talking a partner out of what he or she is feeling with logic. Common comments are: "You shouldn't feel that way," or "Come on, cheer up," or "You're blowing this all out of proportion." In the face of such logical suggestions, the partner may end up feeling guilty for having the emotions and then try to pretend that all is resolved. When truly effective communication happens, both partners feel that they have permission to feel and express whatever they need to, without being stifled by somebody who is afraid to deal with real feelings. Sexual problems often grow out of situations where two people fool themselves into thinking that some rough spots have been logically resolved, but everything is still cooking at a slow boil under the surface.

Network difficulties

In my work as a sex therapist, I have become convinced that one of the major causes of most sexual difficulties that affect two partners is messed-up communication. That may mean that there is a lack of communication or that the communication is inadequate. *An essential key to a full and satisfying sex life for men is knowing how to communicate effectively with partners.* That doesn't mean that you have to be an extrovert or full of social graces. It doesn't mean that you have to be a great conversationalist or even talk a whole lot. It also doesn't mean that you have to have a long and involved relationship with the partner. What it does mean is that you care enough about yourself, your partner, and what you can have together to put some effort into communicating. The next part of this chapter focuses on how to do that.

SPEAK FOR YOURSELF

It is possible to learn the basics of communication and to put them to work for you in all aspects of your life, including your sexual life. I have seen plenty of males who were constantly unsatisfied with sex, and whose relationships fell apart, simply because they were unwilling to put some energy into communication. Many of them actually believed that communicating wasn't masculine. They preferred to ignore the unmanliness of being irresponsible and of being too scared to face the reality of their own feelings.

Speaking for yourself includes more than words. We also "speak" with our eyes, facial expressions, tone of voice, and body movements. In fact, when our words are not fully in agreement with what is going on inside, our faces and body language will often give us away. We also communicate more than ideas. Our feelings, values, and attitudes are a constant part of our messages to other people.

Opening up

Stop reading for a few minutes and give some thought to the conditions that help you open up to another person. Think about the people with whom you feel especially comfortable talking. Think about the last time you really "opened up" to someone, if you have ever been able to do so. What were your surroundings? What kinds of qualities did that other person have? What did you do to help the process along? Think about your responses to these questions before going on to the next paragraph.

Research has shown that there are certain qualities you must have if others are to open up to you, or you to them. They are the qualities that you can seek out in the people you want to become closer to. They are basic to the kind of communication that helps couples have a good sex life together and to work together on improving sexual functioning. Consider how well you can put these into operation with others. Also look at how well you and your partner are able to show them to one another in your efforts at communicating.

Warmth and caring. There probably isn't going to be much communication between two people who don't care about each other at least a little. But there also isn't much communicated between two individuals who care a whole lot about one another but just don't show it. Many married men seem to fall into what I call the "Post-Honeymoon Slump." These are men who have gone through all of the niceties of courting and loving their women. Yet, as soon as the honeymoon is over, they return to a male mold that requires a certain distance between them and their wives. They become less demonstrative about their caring. Bill put it this way: "She got me married, and I wouldn't have done it if I didn't love her. So why should I have to slobber over her all the time now?" He missed the point. Everyone needs reassurance that someone else cares, and everyone needs to feel human warmth. Did you ever try talking to someone who was cold and distant? You probably felt either like shutting up or keeping your conversation on a very superficial level. To open up, you must feel some honest warmth and caring from the other person.

Understanding feelings. It feels terrific when you can talk to someone who really can identify and accept what you are feeling. Everybody has the ability to walk a mile in the other guy's shoes if he wants to make the effort. We've all experienced a lot of emotions—maybe for different reasons, but the feelings are all there. I was working recently with a couple who were having some serious sexual difficulties and found that the major hang-up was in their communication patterns. They never tried to understand and accept each other's feelings. When one of them said something like "I really hope you enjoy sex tonight," the other would respond with "If I don't, you'll hear about it." We worked to get them better attuned to the emotions going on in both of them. That first statement, for example, could be loaded with anxiety and a desire to please the partner. If that partner could respond with an expression of understanding, it could make a world of difference in the communication process and their sex life. A response such as "It sounds as if you are feeling worried that things won't be okay," followed by some reassuring words, could open the doors to much better sexual communication and a far more relaxed sexual encounter.

Being genuine. Here is another key quality that must be part of the foundation for good communication. I had known Greg for many years but somehow never felt close to him. He was a very outgoing person and talked about feelings a great deal. He talked about liking me and wanting me as a friend. It puzzled me that I didn't feel more able to be open with him, so I thought through what it was about him that put me off. I realized that his words just didn't ring true somewhere in my gut. Greg was always trying to get me involved in buying something or in some "big" business deal, and that left me feeling used. I never could quite believe that he was being a real person—being genuine—with me. Being genuine means being willing to bring up the negative feelings and ideas as well as the positive. I can't imagine a genuine human being who doesn't get mad, doesn't have some strong beliefs and values, or who isn't disgusted by some things. But being genuine isn't a license to hurt other people either. You can let your true feelings show without deliberately being mean or spiteful.

Making sense and listening. It is awfully easy for words to be misunderstood and for communication to get garbled. I'm amazed as I listen to partners talking to each other in my office at how often they misunderstand what is being said. Too often we make assumptions about what the other person means, or we're so busy thinking about what we're going to say next that we forget to listen at all. Effective communication demands that we word our ideas as carefully as possible and that we *work* to understand what the other person *means*. It requires asking questions often to clarify meanings whenever we're not quite certain what the other person meant. Too often we're afraid we're going to look stupid just by saying that we don't understand what someone meant. Let a couple of those opportunities to ask questions go by, and you're on your way to a big misunderstanding.

Sense of equality. For good opening up to occur between two people, they both must share the feeling that they are really equal. It is difficult to feel fully comfortable communicating openly and honestly with someone we believe to be on another intelligence level or in some way "better" than ourselves. That applies in relationships as well. If one partner is always in some dominant leadership position in the relationship and the other partner is the submissive follower, these roles will be reflected in their communication with one another. Good communication requires a recognition that everyone has ups and downs, and that each of us sometimes needs more than at other times. Two people working at communication must feel relatively equal to one another if their work is going to pay off in positive results.

No snap judgments. One of the biggest problems in human communication is the tendency to jump to conclusions and make snap judgments. Yet most people open up best to those who are not overanxious to judge them. Larry's wife, Sara, tried to explain to him how she was having difficulty enjoying sex because she so seldom experienced orgasm. Larry immediately jumped to the conclusion that there were serious problems in their relationship and she didn't really love him anymore. Sara said to me, "I just can't talk to him. He has everything figured out for himself before I even have a chance to explain my true feelings." Then there are the more subtle judgments that people put on each other in everyday conversation. The man who is shy and has trouble looking others in the eye is judged to be shifty and untrustworthy. Or the remark meant as a joke is taken to be an insult. And finally, there are value judgments you make about others. Some people assume that their beliefs and values are the "right" ones and judge people who don't agree with them or abide by them as "bad," "wrong," "sinful," or "sick." This is particularly true in the area of sexual preferences and behaviors. People are often quick to judge sexual activities that are different from those they feel are right for themselves. What all this adds up to is that being with someone who can listen openly and be relatively nonjudgmental helps anyone to feel more like opening up.

Trust and respect. Nobody can share of themselves with someone who isn't trusted. You talk about your emotions only to someone you know will accept what you say and treat it with care. I don't want to be laughed at, thought foolish, or told that I shouldn't feel what I know I'm feeling. I can let my feelings out only to someone who will listen, care, and accept me for what I am. Trust also means knowing that what I tell another person will be treated confidentially and not spread to other people without my permission. How can you be absolutely sure you can trust someone? You can't. There is always an element of risk in any human relationship. Anytime you communicate deeply and honestly, you can be hurt, but to get all the good things out of love and sharing, you must accept that risk. You learn to trust your own intuitions about other people to minimize your risks. Sometimes people let you down, but it is usually worth the risk. You also open up best when you are treated with respect. It is pretty difficult to talk to someone who isn't really listening, who seems hurried and anxious to get away, or who wants to do all the talking. So to stimulate good communication, both partners must try to be trustworthy and respectful of one another.

This list of qualities necessary for good communication could probably go on and on. But the qualities discussed in the last few pages are the ones that seem to be important to nearly everyone. They represent the characteristics that can truly stimulate the opening-up process that is so essential to a growing, healthy sexual relationship. That doesn't mean that two partners must "tell all" to each other. Each of us has the right to have areas of privacy within ourselves. But if the boundaries around those areas become barriers to honesty and expression of feelings, they may begin building brick walls that will prevent the full enjoyment of shared sex.

Talking together about sex

A male student who was part of a group discussion on sexuality stated his belief that "sex is something you *do* with each other; you shouldn't have to *talk* about it." That philosophy would be fine if people were just walking penises and vaginas who slipped in and out of sexual encounters. However, people have thoughts, feelings, and needs that often must get out to one another. Sex is one of the most difficult things for most people to talk about, especially if they are worried about their own sexuality.

From the time we were very young, most of us learned that sex was not a subject to be brought up in "polite" company. Traditionally, girls have learned that they shouldn't appear interested enough in sex to talk about it, and boys have learned that sex is okay to joke about, but serious sex talk might make it look as if you don't know something. Fortunately, these stereotyped attitudes have been changing, but there are still many people who are extremely uncomfortable talking about sex.

You may find it relatively easy to discuss your values concerning sex and marriage, how society should treat homosexuals, the "best" forms of birth control, and other "idea topics." When it comes to your own sexual needs and activities, though, even lovers often cannot talk together. Take the subject of masturbation, for example. Most studies have shown that nearly all adults masturbate occasionally throughout their lifetimes. Sex therapists recognize masturbation to be an excellent way of working on the improvement of some aspects of sexual functioning. Yet most of the couples who come to me for help with their sexual concerns have never been able to talk to each other about masturbation. The fact that they each masturbate is often the deep dark secret they have always hidden from each other. A woman once told me how shocked she had been to walk into the bedroom and find her embarrassed husband masturbating. The husband, who sat in my office as she revealed her story, actually hung his head in shame. They were surprised to learn that most adults—married or single, sexually satisfied or frustrated—masturbate. In the week before their next session with me, the couple talked about masturbation together for the first time in their ten-year relationship. The woman finally admitted to her husband somewhat sheepishly that she frequently masturbated herself. They came in for the next meeting feeling much more relaxed and happy that they no longer needed to hide such a significant part of their individual sexual lives.

When people have continuing functional problems during sexual contacts—lack of orgasm, failure to become aroused, discomfort, or inadequate ejaculatory control, for example—they simply must learn how to talk about what they are feeling and what is happening. Bluffing your way along and pretending it doesn't matter won't work if you want to prevent further problems. Fears, anxieties, embarrassments, and all of the other feelings that can help spoil sex need to get discussed, or they may become a part of a vicious circle that will hamper sexual enjoyment at every turn.

The ground rules for sexual communication

At one point or another in any relationship that includes or may include sexual activity, the people involved will need to talk about sex. A responsible male should understand how to participate in the process of sexual communication. First, be aware of the following preliminary ground rules:

1. Pick the right location for talking.

   Where you talk may be important. Both of you should be able to feel relaxed and comfortable, physically as well as emotionally. Sometimes, bed is the ideal place, but it may also be too loaded a situation for some kinds of talking. Beware of atmospheres that encourage superficial conversation and games. Bars and parties are rarely the right place for real communication to take place. You take the initiative. Ask your partner where she or he would feel most comfortable talking, and be certain you feel okay there too.

2. Know your own values.

   Before you set out to communicate about sex, it is a good idea to do some careful thinking about where you stand on some of the value issues related to what you'll be discussing. Know your own beliefs, while letting yourself be open to the attitudes and values of the other person.

3. Find out if both of you are on equal ground.

Always keep in mind that feeling equal is usually essential to any kind of communication. It is even more important when the topic is sex. Both of you may have to examine your feelings about each other and your relationship to determine whether or not you feel equal in the truly significant areas.

4. Make sure you trust each other.

Sex is often unsuccessful when there is lack of trust between the two partners. Likewise, trust must be present between people who are going to discuss sex. Sexual talk is deeply personal; our sexual feelings and fears are intimate and private parts of ourselves. You won't feel much like sharing them unless you trust the other person. You may have to "test the water" a few times to get the right approach.

5. Know what you expect from each other.

Relationships in which sex is discussed may exist on many different levels. There is the casual, uninvolved encounter where two people who know only first names want to find out from each other what feels good. On the other end of the scale is the long-term loving involvement where discussing sex is continually necessary to assure mutual satisfaction. Know which level you are on, and what expectations exist between the two of you before attempting sexual communication.

Getting into it

Once you actually start talking about sex, or anything important, there are some action guidelines to keep in mind. The more you are able to put these guidelines to work for you, the more successful the outcome will be. Remember also that you can make some mistakes in communication, but that when two people care enough to keep going, they will eventually get back on an even keel. Try it and you'll see what I mean. Here are the things to keep foremost in your mind:

1. Be ready to work.

    Communicating honestly about sex takes energy. You may begin to feel tired, frustrated, or hopeless at times. Hang in there until you begin to feel that more progress is being made. Take a break if you need a breather. Time out may give you a chance to think, which will yield a whole new perspective. Good communication is not always pleasant, but with effort the results will usually be worth whatever has to go into the process.

2. Listen and really hear.

    Part of the trusting, caring, and working that must go on between two people involves listening. Learn how to really tune in so that you're not just listening to words but *hearing meanings*. Stop worrying about what you are going to say next. There is no need to defend yourself or invent a clever quip that will be just the right thing to say. You cannot respond effectively until you fully understand what your partner is saying to you. So listen and hear, and ask questions when you don't understand something. Then figure out what you want to say.

3. Don't let silence scare you.

    If you are frightened of silence, you'll stop listening so you can get your own response ready, and you'll start filling the air with useless words. Take your time together. Sometimes when words are inadequate, touching may be the most effective way to communicate. Or your eyes may do some of the talking. But you cannot *not* communicate. There are messages in everything, even silence. Learn to make use of them.

4. Let each other feel whatever needs to be felt.

    Feelings don't have to make logical sense. You don't have to explain or justify them. When you are hearing another's feelings, be careful not to try to talk him or her out of those feelings. Each of you has the right to any feeling and the right not to be talked out of it. Don't try to sweep feelings under the rug, either. Don't resort to tricks such as saying, "It's all over now, so what difference does it make?" Whenever the feelings are still there, it makes a difference and there may be more work to do.

5. Beware of the "I don't want to hurt you" cop-out.

Some of the most important sex-related discussions get put aside because one partner is afraid of hurting the other. What they are usually afraid of is facing the consequences of the partner's discomfort. Any lasting relationship is bound to have some hurt in it, and people must trust one another enough to hope that the hurts will not do serious long-term damage to the relationship. But to avoid important communication out of the fear of hurting someone is bound to get you into trouble eventually. So don't cop out on someone you care about.

Dealing with sexual problems through communication

The real test of sexual communication comes in the clinches, when there is a problem to be resolved. Whenever that involves another person, you will need to bring all of your communication skills into action. However, dealing with problems may require some further special consideration.

For one thing, don't hurry to solve a problem. It usually takes time to get into a mess, and so it takes time to get out of one. Resist the urge to "just get it over with." That is a sure way to miss something important in your communication. Be certain to talk out all of your negative feelings until you can feel their tension gone from your insides. Usually that will take some time.

Resolving sexual problems between you and another person may also require some degree of compromise. If two people enter into problem-solving communication with the attitude that neither one of them will budge an inch, not much is going to happen. This is where power struggles can be so dangerous. There will always have to be some give and take in working on sexual problems, but both of you should be comfortable with how much you give or take. It is that need for equality again.

Be careful to resolve your own personal difficulties as much as possible before trying to involve a partner in the process. If you have some personal hang-up with sex or women or anything else, your partner isn't going to be of much help until you've faced the problem and know where you stand on it. Don't lay something on the other person that is really your own problem—although after working on it yourself for a while, it may be good to let your partner know where you are and how you can be helped with it.

Finally, know when to seek outside help in communication. Two people can sometimes get so bogged down in feelings, misunderstandings, and games that they lose their perspective. As couples struggle to work things out together sexually, they may begin to feel as if they are going in circles or that they always come up against the same brick wall. An outside perspective may help. An understanding friend who can avoid taking sides may be the answer. Other times a professional counselor or sex therapist should be consulted (see Chapter 7). In any case, it is a sign of real strength and maturity to know when you have exhausted your own resources and to seek some outside ideas.

SEXUAL RESPONSIBILITY

Vic was a young man who had locked himself into several patterns that kept him from exercising responsibility for his own sexual enjoyment. He was unmarried and for about ten years had had sexual encounters with many partners. During those encounters he often found he ejaculated sooner than he wanted or had trouble keeping his erection. Each time he had a problem, he fell back on one of his sexual "blame games." He blamed either himself or his partner for the lack of sexual success. Sometimes he worried about himself: "What is wrong with me?" The rest of the time he would find something in his partner to blame. He would tell himself, "What a dog! No wonder I couldn't get it up." Either way he was the real loser. When he blamed himself, he was filled with guilt and anxiety that simply set him up for more failure the next time. When he blamed his partner, he lost the opportunity to face his problems squarely and do something about them.

When Vic first consulted me, we worked to get him to realize that the only one responsible for his sexual pleasure —or lack of it—was himself. *He* had to choose sexual partners who appealed to him and had to cultivate the kind of relationship that would lead to pleasurable sex. It was not his partner's job to give him an erection, an orgasm, or a well-timed sexual experience.

During our first counseling session, I ran into another of the sexual roadblocks that Vic had invented. He was a strong believer that sex is one of those parts of life that should come naturally. It is true that penises get erect and vaginas get wet, usually without much difficulty. And appropriate stimulation will generally trigger an orgasm. However, like any other human activity, to develop the most pleasurable sexual peaks and to get the highest sexual rewards, the means to sexual pleasure must be learned, practiced, and perfected. At first, Vic felt that it was a sign of inadequacy and immaturity to do some of the at-home exercises that I suggested to him. After he reluctantly gave some of them a try, he began reporting back to me that he understood what sexual responsibility was all about. He was learning more about his sexual responses and how to control them.

There are other aspects of sexual responsibility as well. Good communication demands that you trust your partner and be trustworthy yourself. It also means that sometimes you will have to face and deal with negative and hurtful feelings along with the positive and pleasing ones. Another important aspect of responsibility in male-female sex is birth control, discussed in Chapter 8.

The point is that good sex may be developed with the proper knowledge and a little effort. It doesn't take long to get yourself into a pleasurable cycle in which sex usually works well and feels good. Then you can relax and look forward to the next time, which builds up even more good feelings. The occasional problems and failures can be put into perspective so you are not depressed whenever they occur.

The next several chapters of this book offer you some specific exercises that can put you more deeply in touch with your own body, develop your awareness of your own sexual responsiveness, and help with particular sexual problems. The responsibility for what you get out of these exercises is yours, but the chances are very good that they can work for you.

MORE COMMUNICATION EXERCISES

Working on communication: an exercise for two

Before trying to improve your patterns of communication, both of you should read this entire chapter. Start by rating each other on the following qualities. Write your answers on separate sheets of paper without first discussing the rating scale or qualities with each other. When you have both finished your ratings, read on.

RATING SCALE:

4 = Tops. He/she does a great job
of showing this quality to me.
3 = Okay. Most of the time I feel
this from him/her.
2 = Fair. I could really stand to have
more of this quality from her/him.
1 = Poor. I rarely, if ever, feel this
from her/him.

RATING OF YOUR PARTNER	QUALITIES IN YOUR PARTNER
_____	Caring and consideration toward me.
_____	Ability to show warmth and love.
_____	Sensitivity and understanding toward my emotions.
_____	Lets me feel whatever I need to feel, without trying to talk me out of it.
_____	Seems to listen and really hear what I mean.
_____	Acts real and honest with me so that I can feel that he/she is being genuine.
_____	Says things so that they make sense and I can understand him/her.
_____	Seems to feel on an equal level with me in the areas that are important to me.
_____	Doesn't jump to conclusions or make snap judgments about me or others.
_____	Treats me with respect.
_____	Is trustworthy.
_____	Seems to trust me and shares inner feelings and thoughts with me.

When you have both finished your ratings, exchange them so that you each may take a look at how you were rated by the other. However, you both should agree to the following:

1. Do not talk about your reactions to the ratings for *fifteen minutes*, during which time you should:
    a. Think about why your partner might have rated you as he or she did. Assume that the ratings represent honest reactions.
    b. Think about which ratings made you feel best and which made you feel worst.
    c. Ask yourself if you were surprised by any of the ratings. Why or why not?

d. Look beneath any anger you might feel or any need to "defend" yourself against a rating. If you are hurt, be ready to admit it. Keep in mind that your partner had a right to rate you in any manner that seemed honest to her or him. It can lead to a deeper understanding.

2. When you are ready to start talking together about your mutual ratings:
   a. You should agree on the most comfortable location.
   b. Share only your own feelings and reactions, being careful not to make assumptions and judgments about your partner's feelings or motivations.
   c. After one of you has had a chance to make a point, the other should spend some time summarizing what was heard, so you can be sure that you are hearing each other accurately. Clear up any misunderstandings that your partner has about anything you have said. Give each other time to do this.

Now, where do you go from here? If this exercise has shown you ways to improve your ability to communicate, are you ready to work toward that goal? Check out the ideas in this chapter and decide whether or not you think the two of you could work on particular areas. The remainder of the book will help you to understand and communicate about your sexual relationship better. If you think you might need counseling from a professional, consult the guidelines in Chapter 7.

You might want to compare notes on the next exercise too. Read through it and decide together.

What can you talk about?
This exercise can help you be aware of your ease or lack of it in talking to others about sex. Some sexual topics will make you stutter or blush, often because they hit too close to home. Most of us feel comfortable with some areas, however, at least when talking to certain people.

In the following three columns, make a check if you would

feel able to discuss that particular topic, *in detail*, with the person indicated:

Your spouse or lover	Your closest male friend	Your closest female friend	Topics
————	————	————	Your sex education as a teenager.
————	————	————	Your first sexual experience with another person.
————	————	————	The first time you masturbated.
————	————	————	Your present frequency and methods of masturbation.
————	————	————	Your most persistent sexual fantasies.
————	————	————	Any homosexual feelings you have experienced.
————	————	————	Homosexual activity in which you have participated.
————	————	————	The "kinkiest" sexual interests you have.
————	————	————	Your degree of interest in oral sex.
————	————	————	The sexual experience in your past you feel most guilty about.
————	————	————	The parts of your body you like and dislike most.
————	————	————	Your values and preferences concerning birth control.

After you have finished deciding which topics you could talk over with various people, look back over your check marks and ask yourself the following questions:

1. What is it about that person that enables you to feel comfortable discussing sexual topics with him or her?

2. Are you able to give the person back the same kinds of feelings so that she or he feels able to talk about sex with you?

3. Note the areas that you would *not* feel able to discuss. Why not? What sorts of feelings would keep you from talking about the topic?

4. Would you like to discuss any of the taboo topics with somebody? If so, perhaps some of the other parts of this chapter may offer you some suggestions.

Talking about masturbation

I am firmly convinced that for many couples, establishing good communication about masturbation may be a major step toward improving sexual communication generally and working on the improvement of shared sex. Some couples talk about masturbation easily, while others never dare to bring up the subject with each other. If you are going to be trying some of the sexual exercises in the next few chapters with a partner, I suggest that you experiment with this exercise first. It may lower some important communication barriers and move you closer to a more satisfying sex life.

1. Make sure your partner has read at least the opening chapters of this book, including the preceding paragraph. If he or she would prefer not to do all or any part of this exercise, that is his or her choice. If you both choose to go ahead, read on.

2. Before talking about masturbation at all, take a few minutes right now to tell each other how you feel about trying this exercise. Just stick to your feelings, and don't get into long explanations of *why* you're feeling them. Deal with

emotion words such as *embarrassed, nervous, scared, turned on,* or *anticipating.*

3. Start off under the assumption that you both masturbate. Most adults do. If you don't, that's okay too, and you may answer the following questions accordingly. Take turns telling each other the answers to these questions as honestly as possible:

   a. How frequently, on the average, do you masturbate?

   b. Do you generally find it to be an enjoyable activity, physically and emotionally?

   c. In the past or present, have you experienced guilt or other negative feelings because of masturbation? If so, why?

   d. How do you feel about your partner talking about his or her masturbating (or not masturbating)? Are you surprised or uncomfortable in any way? Talk together about how you feel at this point in the exercise.

   e. What are your two or three favorite methods of masturbation? Describe them with as much detail as you feel comfortable.

   f. Would you (or do you) feel comfortable masturbating in the presence of your partner? Explain how this might make you feel.

   g. Would you (or do you) enjoy watching your partner masturbate? Explain your feelings about this.

4. When you both feel ready for this part of the exercise, give it a try. Lie down next to each other, fully clothed, on a bed or on the floor. Don't look at each other, either by having the room darkened or by closing your eyes. Then, both of you should make sounds as if you are masturbating (don't actually masturbate). Breathe, move, and make vocal sounds as you would if you were masturbating. You may feel silly and like laughing over this too, so go ahead. Build your sounds as if you were experiencing orgasm. Don't look at each other until you are both "finished"

and have quieted down. Now, talk over how the whole experience made you feel.

What to do about sex problems

If sex is always completely satisfactory for you and your partner, there is probably no point in doing this exercise. However, if you are a man and things don't always go as you would like sexually, give this section a try. It may help you understand better what is happening to you.

1. Begin by answering the following questions:
    a. What is the most troublesome thing that happens for you or your partner during sex?
    b. When was the last time this bothered you?
    c. How did this last experience make you feel?
    d. Did you and your partner talk over the problem?

2. If the problem involved the failure of your sex organs to function as you wished, look at the following possibilities. During the last time or two the problem bothered you:
    a. Did you *really* want to have sex at that time?
    b. Were you depressed, anxious, or fatigued?
    c. Was your partner desirable and sexually attractive to you?
    d. Did you trust and feel comfortable with the partner?
    e. Did you and your partner have trouble letting each other know what felt good and what you wanted from each other?
    f. Were you and your partner feeling disappointed with each other or your relationship in any way?
    g. Did you and your partner seem to do anything to deliberately turn one another off?

If you answered *yes* to any of these questions, perhaps it would do some good to take a closer look at what is going on in your own life or in your relationship that may be helping to spoil your sexual encounters. The ideas in this chapter may offer you some suggestions for establishing better lines of communication between you and your partner. That is an essential beginning. Other chapters in this book may give you more specific help. Here are some guidelines to help you find the most appropriate chapters:

If you have been having difficulty controlling when you reach orgasm and often end up ejaculating sooner than you wish, see Chapters 3 and 4.

If you sometimes have trouble keeping your erection during sex, see Chapters 3 and 5.

If you sometimes cannot have an orgasm when you want to, and you have to try especially hard to get one, see Chapters 3 and 6.

If you think alcohol, drugs, or your physical health are interfering with your enjoyment of sex, see Chapter 6.

If you lack interest in sex and wish you had more, see Chapter 6.

If the problem seems to be largely your partner's, see Chapter 7.

If you think you need outside professional help with your sexual problems, see Chapter 7.

3

~——•——~

Using
What You've Got

The chances are good that if you haven't mastered some of the basics of communication described in the last chapter, sharing sex with another person will never be as complete or satisfying as it could be. Another important way of helping to ensure good sex is by getting thoroughly acquainted with your own body's sexual qualities. This chapter is going to focus on helping you find what you've got, use it, and feel good about it.

My first suggestion is that you really look at your body, identify all the parts of your sex organs, and begin to touch— and really *feel*—all parts of your body. At first it may all seem strange or embarrassing to you. When I gave these suggestions to a thirty-year-old man who was a client of mine in sex therapy, he began to get really angry. "Do you think I'm some kind of fairy?" he snapped. "I'm not going to get a mirror to look at my body, or lie around touching myself. There must be other ways to do this!"

Men are often uncomfortable about spending too much time examining or handling their own bodies, especially their sex organs, or at least that other people should know about it. For some reason, they associate this kind of behavior with vanity, or they assume that it has something to do with homosexuality.

In fact there are many people who mistakenly believe that some men become homosexuals by spending too much time on their own bodies. Others believe that if a man enjoys touching his penis and masturbating, it must mean that he is homosexual. These opinions are incorrect. The exercises found in this chapter have nothing to do with your sexual preferences, whether homosexual, heterosexual, bisexual, or something else. The exercises are for people with male bodies.

Let's face it. Most men are very curious about their bodies and the way they compare to those of other men. They wonder about muscles and chest size, the relative size of the penis, how the testicles hang, the hair line, height, weight, and so on. They sneak long looks at themselves in the mirror when they get the chance. And they feel themselves, hold on to their genitals in bed, and touch their skin and body hair. They also sneak looks at other men's bodies, including their penises, when they get the chance, in shower rooms, standing next to each other at urinals, or at the beach, usually not lingering long enough to be noticed. What's more, all that looking—at themselves and at others—is perfectly natural and healthy.

Only too often, though, they get upset by what they see. Jerry was a college student who was worried about two problems. First, whenever he was in a men's room, he found it difficult, or even impossible, to urinate while standing next to another man. More seriously, he was having difficulty getting an erection during his attempts at sex. It didn't take Jerry long to admit that his major concern had always been the size of his penis. "My cock is smaller than anybody's," he moaned. "I can't ever expect to really satisfy a woman. I thought it would grow some more, but I guess by now it's about as big as it'll ever be." This concern was at the root of his other problems. His insecurity in the men's room wouldn't allow him to relax enough to urinate. His insecurity in bed wouldn't allow him to get started with sex because he was so afraid of failure.

After talking more about his worries, and after trying some of the exercises in this chapter, Jerry began to feel better, largely because he realized that his fear was unfounded and that his penis was not smaller than anyone else's. With this realization, and with some further work, his urinary and sexual problems began to fade.

GETTING IN TOUCH WITH YOUR BODY

To feel really good about sex, and be sure that your shared sexual contacts are fully satisfying, you must first know and feel good about your body. Try doing all the exercises at some point, but read each section through before actually attempting the activities. However, feel free to skip any part that makes you uncomfortable. Maybe you'll feel more like coming back to these exercises some other time.

Do one "step" at a time, moving to the next step only when you feel ready to do so. You may want to repeat some steps one or more times.

Step 1—looking at yourself
Many men have found these exercises helpful in getting better acquainted and more relaxed with their bodies and sexual feelings. You may want to start by taking a hot and relaxing shower or bath.

In a private place, where you can feel comfortable, relaxed, and free from interruptions, remove all of your clothing. (Some men find that they are more comfortable with these exercises in subdued light or with their favorite music as background.) Try to have a large mirror available so that you can stand back and take a look at your entire body, or at least most of it. Spend some time looking at each part of your body, beginning with your head and moving downward. Think about which parts you particularly like and which you dislike. The following questions may help:

1. Your head. How do you feel about your hair? Your eyes, nose, and ears? Do you like your teeth and lips? What

about your chin? Your beard? Do you wish you had more facial hair?

2. Your neck, shoulders, arms, and hands. How do they look to you? Are they muscular enough? Too skinny? Too stubby? Do they move freely and comfortably?

3. Your torso and back. Are they wide enough? Muscular enough? Deep enough? Too hairy or not hairy enough? Does your stomach stick out?

4. Your genitals. What is your general reaction to them? Too small? Just right? Further exercise will focus on them in more detail.

5. Your butt. Does it stick out too much? Is it rounded? Flat? Too fat? Too thin?

6. Your legs. Do you like them? Are they too skinny? Too fat? How do you feel about the hair on them?

Ask yourself, in a more general way, what things about your body you would most like to change. Move around as you watch yourself in the mirror. Pull in your stomach. Flex your muscles. Slouch. Make faces. Stand up straight.

Now, sit or recline, and prop up a mirror in front of you so that you have a close-up view of your sex organs. I want you to identify your sexual parts with the help of the drawing on page 65. You have probably noticed since the time of puberty, when your sex organs matured, that the skin on them tends to be somewhat darker than the skin on other parts of your body.

Hold your penis and look at it. The rounded, thicker end is called the *glans*. If you have not been circumcised, the glans is partially or wholly covered by the *foreskin* or *prepuce*, so you may want to pull this skin back to take a closer look. With circumcision, a surgical operation usually performed on babies, the foreskin has been removed. The ridge around the edge of the glans is called the *corona*, and the thin band of skin on the underside of the glans is called the *frenulum*. Most males find that the frenulum and corona are the most sensitive

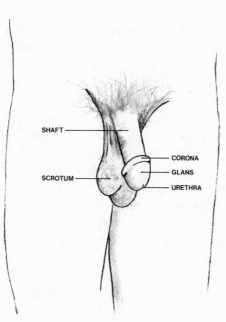

SHAFT

CORONA

GLANS

SCROTUM

URETHRA

parts of the penis and particularly susceptible when touched. (Incidentally, many men find parts of these exercises to be sexually arousing and get erections during them. If you find this happening, don't let it worry you. Just keep going with the exercises.) Near the tip of the glans is the opening out of which urine and semen come. This is the opening of the *urethra*, a tube that runs the entire length of the penis and up into your body. The main part of your penis, extending from the glans and connecting to your body, is called the *shaft*.

The penis is packed with blood vessels, nerves, and tissues that fill with blood to make it erect. Running lengthwise under the skin along the top of the shaft are two parallel columns of this spongy tissue. Each is called a *corpus cavernosum*. If your penis is limp, you may be able to feel them faintly, but they are very easy to see and feel when you have an erection. Along the bottom midline of the penis is a third column of erectile tissue, the *corpus spongiosum*. It is also most noticeable when the penis is fully erect. Contrary to what a lot of people believe, there is no bone or cartilage in the penis. Erection happens when blood builds up in the three columns of spongy tissue.

Men often worry about the shape of their penises as well as the size. Look at yours. It may curve slightly because of the way you have worn it in your underwear for years. The curve doesn't affect its functioning at all. If you're interested, you can measure the length of your penis to the tip of the glans by holding a ruler along the top, with one end up against the body. Most adult men have a nonerect penis that is from 2½ to 4 inches (6 to 10 cm) long, although smaller or larger penises are quite normal. Erection is the great equalizer, since smaller penises gain proportionately more size upon erection than do larger ones. Erect penises are typically 5 to 6½ inches (12 to 17 cm) long, although again there is a wide range of normal variation. Erect penises vary in shape, too, with some thicker, or more pointed, or more curved than others.

Many men, as they look at other men's penises, begin to worry that theirs is smaller. It's a curious fact that when you look down on your own penis, during urination for example, it tends to look smaller than if you were able to see it from the side at a greater distance. A man is apt to see his own penis from the top, while seeing those of other men from the front or side. It is natural that your own appears smaller. Try taking a good look in a mirror at your own side view from a distance. Chances are you'll look pretty much like those other guys you've observed. Even if you don't, it really is beside the point. The measure of a man—sexually and otherwise—has nothing to do with the measurements of his penis. The size also varies with temperature conditions and emotion. When a man is cold, or under some emotional stress, his penis is at its smallest.

After you have explored your penis and its various parts, take a look at your *scrotum*, the bag of skin beneath the penis. This is usually wrinkly skin, and you can feel the two *testes* or *testicles* that are contained inside and are somewhat movable. Note whether your testes are pulled up tight against your body or are hanging loosely in the scrotum. As you surely have noticed, the position of your testes varies with temperature conditions, nervousness, sexual arousal, and other emotional reactions. Cup your scrotum in your hand and think about how this feels. Most men find their scrotums to be highly arousing too. If you stand up and look in a mirror, you will probably notice that one testis hangs lower than the other. This is true for most men. You may at times notice the testes moving around in the scrotum, and this is perfectly normal.

If you look carefully with the mirror under your scrotum, you will see the *perineum*, an area of skin between the attachment of the scrotum and your *anus*. The anus is in close proximity to your genitals. It is not a sex organ, but many men find that the anal region is highly sensitive and may be a part of sexual stimulation. You may wish to touch this area of your body too.

Before moving on to the next step of self-exploration, you may want to repeat Step 1. Don't be too quick to move on; be sure you feel ready. Stop and take stock of how all this made you feel. If you had some negative feelings, take some time to figure out why.

Step 2—touching yourself

It usually feels good to touch ourselves, all over. Babies and children touch themselves a lot, but many are taught that it's not a nice thing to do. I am not advocating that you go around handling yourself all the time, but I have found that many men can function better sexually, and enjoy it more, after learning more about how their bodies feel. Most men seem to think of sex as something that just the sex organs do and feel, rather than realizing that sex can be an experience for the whole body. But first, you have to be familiar with touching, and feeling, the whole body.

You feel your body from the inside as well as the outside. If you stop right now and pay attention to what is going on inside, you probably will notice some tension—perhaps in your neck and shoulders, face and head, abdomen, or back. You may feel tiredness or minor aches here and there. You may feel really strong and healthy. *Stop for a few minutes and try to get in touch with what is going on inside your body. How does it feel?* Don't worry about why you're feeling a certain way, just about what you're feeling.

To *feel* what you touch you must relax. Even though sexual activity makes your body tighten up with sexual tension, the best sex usually happens in an atmosphere of relaxation. After removing all of your clothing in a private place where you won't have to worry about embarrassing interruptions, try the following steps toward relaxing:

1. Lie down on a bed or on the floor, in a position where you will be able to get comfortable and relax all of your body.

2. Tighten up the muscles all over your body. Contract them well. Make fists and put a grimace on your face.

3. Take a deep breath and, as you are letting it out slowly, concentrate on relaxing all of your muscles. Let them go completely slack. Relax your scalp and facial muscles and close your eyes.

4. While lying quietly with your eyes closed, take an inner survey of your muscles. Start with your toes and gradually think about all of your muscle groups, up to the top of your head. Wherever you can detect any tension left, let the muscles relax completely.

5. Take three more good deep breaths, and imagine yourself exhaling any leftover tension with each one.

6. Lie still for a few more minutes, but don't let yourself go to sleep. Then go on to the next step.

Outer body touching is the next part of this exercise. Some people like to use oils or lotions on their skin for this but I usually recommend doing it without anything artificial to alter the way your skin feels naturally. The choice is yours. Do the exercise while you are lying down and feeling relaxed from the earlier relaxation steps, keeping your eyes closed. As you go through it, try to feel with your fingers and skin *and* from inside. Your fingers will detect textures and bumps and curves. You will feel *how* you touch your skin—gently, roughly, painfully. But inside, does it feel good? Do you become tense? Does it tickle? Hurt? Do you dislike it? Does it turn you on sexually? Or turn you off? Give it a try and see for yourself.

Start by touching the hair on top of your head. Feel its texture and length. Then move to your face and touch your eyelids, nose, lips, cheeks, chin, ears. Think about the parts of your face you like best. Move down to your chest and abdomen, feeling their contours and the texture of the skin. Touch your nipples, navel, and whatever hair is found in this area. Incidentally, many men have little or no hair on their chests. Also touch each arm and hand, feeling the muscles and bones under the skin.

When you feel ready, move down to your sex organs. Start with your pubic hair. Feel its texture and springy quality. Then try touching various parts of your penis. Move a finger along the top surface and both sides. Which areas of the shaft seem most sensitive? Spend some time lightly rubbing or stroking the edge of the head of your penis, or glans, trying to find exactly which areas are most sensitive. Try the top, bottom, and sides. Again, don't worry if you find yourself getting an erection; that is a very natural reaction to such stimulation. Hold your whole penis in your hand for a few minutes. Don't move the hand as you would in masturbation, just hold it quietly without any motion. Feel the body heat between your hand and penis. How does your penis feel when enclosed in this manner?

Then move on to your scrotal skin. As lightly and gently as possible, run your fingers over the entire surface of your scrotum. Just barely touch the hairs and skin. You may have the sensation of your testes moving around in the scrotum as a result of this stimulation. Again, it may also cause you to have some erection of the penis. Now press more firmly on the scrotal skin, but not firmly enough to be uncomfortable. Take some of the loose skin between two fingers, and feel for the thickness of the skin. Cupping your fingers around the entire scrotal sac, notice how tightly drawn or loosely hanging it is right now.

After you think that you have sufficiently explored your sexual parts, you may want to spend some time touching your perineum (under the scrotum) and anal region. Start out with a light touch and then increase the pressure to whatever level you wish.

Finally, move your hands over your buttocks (for this you may want to stand or lie on your stomach awhile) and over your inner and outer thighs. Feel the texture and tautness of the skin. Touch the hair on your legs and note how it feels to your fingers. You may also want to explore your knees, shins, and feet.

After this total touching experience has been completed, lie back, close your eyes, and relax your muscles. Take two or three deep breaths. Think about the experience.

> To what parts of your body did you have the most positive reactions? The most negative?

> Did you find any of the touching especially sexually arousing?

> Did you learn anything new about the feel of your body?

> Do you sense any changes in your attitudes toward your body?

Step 3—your body responds

This section is designed to help you get fully in touch with the responses of your body to sexual excitement. It involves producing sexual arousal by manipulating your sex organs and/or other parts of your body, in other words, masturbation. Although most men masturbate with some regularity, some feel that it is inappropriate or wrong for them. If you feel negative about masturbation, read the suggestions without acting on them, because you can apply what you learn to other forms of sexual activity. However, to enjoy shared sexual encounters with a partner fully, a man must feel comfortable with and good about his own body and its sexual responsiveness. Many men have found that these exercises can help them toward that end.

It's important to remember that sexual excitement involves not only the sex organs, but the entire body. The physical response to sexual arousal seems to happen in three stages:

1. *Desire.* Usually, there is a trigger that starts to turn you on. You may see someone who is sexually attractive, or have a sexy thought, or read about something sexy—there are loads of reasons for getting aroused. Sometimes the desire isn't even expressed by your body—it just remains a pleasant thought or emotion. Other times, you progress to the second stage of sexual response:

2. *Tension building.* When you're sexually turned on, your body gradually builds up tension. Blood fills the pelvic area, swelling the penis into an erection and enlarging the testes and scrotal skin. Muscles all over the body tighten, and your heart rate, breathing, and blood pressure increase.

3. *Tension releasing.* If sexual stimulation continues, and your bodily tension builds to a certain peak, the tension is released, triggered by that highly pleasurable orgasm or sexual climax. In men, orgasm is usually accompanied by ejaculation of semen from the penis and discharge of tension from the muscles, resulting in some uncontrolled movement. Then, gradually the body returns to a relaxed and calm state.

Those are the three stages of sexual response on which the following exercises will focus. It's a good idea to read through the entire sequence of activities before actually trying them because it's difficult to stop during sexual excitement to read what the book has to say. Again, these exercises should be carried out in a relaxing place where you won't be interrupted. Remove your clothes and sit or recline in a comfortable position. You may want to watch yourself in a mirror during the exercises; that is up to you.

Desire. Close your eyes and relax as fully as possible. Spend five or ten minutes thinking about the things that most often trigger your sexual desire. Who and what turn you on? What kinds of people or body characteristics? What kinds of fantasies? What kinds of situations and atmospheres? What kinds of smells, tastes, sounds, sights, and touches? Let yourself imagine these turn-ons for a while. You may begin to feel your body responding to these thoughts and fantasies.

Tension building. First stimulate your penis, scrotum, and other body parts in ways that you generally find sexually arousing. Use some sort of lubricant if you wish, such as K-Y jelly, mineral oil, or petroleum jelly. Notice what happens all over your body. Also, try *not to have an orgasm* until you have fully experienced the total body involvement of sexual arousal. If you feel the inner satisfaction that signals you are about to ejaculate, stop all stimulation until the sensation has gone away, then proceed carefully.

Become aware of the way erection affects the size of your penis. Feel its greater length and thickness. Notice the fullness of the glans, which reaches its peak as you near the time of orgasm. Feel for the three columns of spongy tissue that have become hard as they have filled with blood. The two parallel columns of erectile tissue along the upper part harden first, and the single column along the underside of the penis becomes fully hard a little later, along with the glans. When your penis is fully erect, spend some time again tracing a finger along various areas on the shaft and glans to find where the most sensitive areas are. You may assume that you already know, but many men are surprised by new discoveries when they take some time to explore again.

As sexual stimulation continues, you may notice droplets of a clear, sticky liquid forming at the urethral opening on the end of the penis. This is produced by two internal *Cowper's glands* (or bulbourethral glands) and apparently neutralizes acids in the urethra to permit safe passage of the microscopic sperm. When this liquid is secreted in large amounts, it also becomes an effective lubricant. If your penis produces enough of the secretion, you may want to smooth it over your fingers and penis while you continue the stimulation. The more sexual tension builds in your body, the more fully erect your penis becomes. In the later stages, the glans is especially full, and it darkens in color.

After you have felt sexually aroused for a few minutes and your penis is fully erect, spend some time exploring your scrotum. If you touch your scrotum with your fingers and cup it in your hand, you may notice that the entire area feels enlarged. During sexual arousal the scrotal skin itself thickens, and the testes inside increase by up to 50 percent more than their usual size. Try to feel this fullness. You may also be able to feel the testes moving around on their own inside the scrotum. As sexual arousal continues, the testes tend to pull upward toward the body, being pulled up the tightest during orgasm.

Touch your nipples with your fingers to find out whether or not they have become hardened and erect. Nipple erection during sexual arousal occurs in only about one-third of males. About one-fourth develop a "sex flush" when aroused, appearing as a redness of the skin on the upper chest and neck. In especially intense sex, the sex flush may spread to the back, abdomen, and other body areas. There doesn't seem to be any particular relationship between the appearance of nipple hardness or the sex flush and the degree of sexual enjoyment.

Spend some time tuning into what is going on around your entire body. If you're really turned on, you'll probably notice that your heart rate and breathing have speeded up. Your muscles are also tense, and this may lead to some occasional involuntary, jerking motions of your arms, hands, legs, feet, and other body parts. You may feel like moving your entire body around a great deal. On the other hand, some men lie relatively still during sexual arousal. Try to do whatever seems comfortable and spontaneous to you.

If you would prefer not to have an orgasm this time, simply stop stimulating yourself and take a few deep breaths. Although you may feel a little frustrated for a short time, there is really nothing wrong with getting aroused and then not finishing off with an orgasm. Many men can have very enjoyable sexual experiences occasionally without orgasm. Sexual tension gradually dissipates, even without climax. It's a myth that sex without orgasm is always a bad thing. It simply is not the case. You may have heard the story of the turned-on guy who ends up with painful "blue balls" or "lover's nuts" because he doesn't ejaculate. Although very intense arousal for a long time can lead to an aching sensation in the testes and lower abdomen, this is rare and completely harmless if it happens. So, having an orgasm is a matter of choice.

If you do want to have an orgasm in this experience, read through the next section first.

Tension releasing. Sexual tension goes away rapidly after orgasm. Typically when men get close to orgasm, their body movements become more intense and their stimulation on the penis increases. If you can manage to slow down a little, you will be able to feel your body building up to orgasm. When you know you're getting close to ejaculating, taper off your stimulation just a little. Try to identify that inner sensation that tells you that orgasm is about to happen. If you are good at sensing that point, you can also learn how to delay orgasm, if you choose to do so (see Chapter 4). At this point, if you want, you can stop the stimulation briefly and then begin again. Before long, the orgasm warning signal will return. When you feel like it, go ahead, let go, and enjoy your orgasm as much as possible.

These are the things that happen when you reach your climax. The most obvious feelings are the inner contractions of your ejaculatory muscles and the throbbing contractions of your penis. These contractions expel spurts of semen from the penis. The first three or four contractions are the strongest and push out the greatest amounts of semen. Gradually, the contractions get weaker and farther apart, until the last drops of semen have been squeezed out.

Of all the stages of sexual response, orgasm involves the

entire body most completely. Your breathing increases so that you are nearly panting, and your heart races. If you really let yourself go, your entire body will probably writhe and jerk around to some extent. Your pelvis will typically make thrusting movements during the orgasm. You may open your mouth or make a grimace, and sometimes you may gasp, groan, or yell. Yet, don't worry about copying this description to make it look good. Just allow your body to do "what comes naturally."

The one thing that is really almost impossible to describe is the overall pleasurable feeling that fills your entire body during orgasm. I'll simply assume that each man who reads this book will know what I am talking about.

The entire orgasm, down to the last contractions of the penis, does not last more than twenty to thirty seconds. You may feel several pleasant "aftershocks" during that period. Orgasm is usually followed by some heavy breathing and a feeling of relaxation through the entire body. Almost immediately you begin to lose your erection. About half is lost right away, and then your penis may stay semihard for a while longer. It is quite common for some perspiration to appear on the skin following orgasm. Quite rapidly, your pulse rate and breathing return to normal. Usually, people feel calm, relaxed, and somewhat drowsy.

Thinking it over.   When you have completed Step 3, whether or not you have had an orgasm, spend a few minutes relaxing and thinking over your reactions. Here are some questions that might help you assess how you feel about experiencing the sexual responses of your body:

> Did you feel self-conscious about any of the exercises you have done?

> Which stage(s) of sexual arousal did you enjoy most? Why?

> What new things did you learn about your body or emotions during sexual response?

> If you experienced an orgasm, how did you feel after?

Did you feel happy and satisfied, or somewhat guilty or unfulfilled?

Is there anything that could have made this experience any better for you?

Did being alone affect your level of enjoyment of the experience at all? Did it help you to be more spontaneous and really "let go"? Or did it all seem rather flat and lifeless? If the latter is true, be sure to read the next section.

Step 4—expanding your enjoyment with fantasy

An important part of nearly everyone's sex life is *fantasy*. We often find ourselves daydreaming about the people who turn us on or the sexual things we would like to be able to do. Sometimes we have surprising sexual fantasies about sexual activities that really don't appeal to us very much or that we would never think of actually doing.

Dave confided to me that sometimes when he was masturbating or sharing sex with his wife, he would indulge himself in his favorite sexual fantasy. Here it is:

> I like to imagine that I have been captured by three beautiful women. All of them have really great bodies. They strip me naked and tie my hands and feet so that I am stretched out on the floor. After they look me over, they get really turned on and take off all their clothes. (They're wearing tight space woman uniforms.) Then they take turns working me over sexually. They lick me from head to toe and stimulate every part of me until I'm practically wild.
>
> After I'm really turned on, they bring in this big guy who is also nude. They force him to give me a blow job, which I try not to like but really do. They stand around and watch as he's going down on me. Then they send him away and go back to work on me themselves.
>
> It doesn't take long before I have a really tremendous

climax that shakes my whole body and knocks one of the women down. That's where the fantasy usually ends.

Dave really enjoyed his fantasy whenever he used it and was not at all worried about the man in it. His only concern was that the fantasy might be "childish." I assured him that he wasn't alone in his active fantasy life. Some men are embarrassed that they have sexual daydreams or assume that the fantasies are a sign of sexual frustration. Usually, sexual fantasies are simply pleasant images that can make sex more intense and more fun. The same is true for sexy photo magazines, movies, books, or music. They often get us fantasizing about sex, and we project ourselves into the scene. Letting our imaginations go can be another way of expanding sexual enjoyment.

Some couples develop enough trust in one another so that they can tell each other about their sexual fantasies. That may be good for a laugh, or it may lead to some good sex together. Some sexual partners have fun acting out their fantasies together. This can be done by playing certain roles in the bedroom, or by acting out rather elaborate scenes. About twice a year, one married couple I know would go out separately and meet in a cheap tavern. They would pretend they were meeting at the bar for the first time, eventually leaving and going to a nearby motel. They would spend the night there and have sex. They claimed that this was a refreshing occasional change for their sex life that was fun and doubled as a short vacation from home.

How far you go with your sexual fantasies is up to you, providing no one gets hurt. You may feel that you don't have a very active imagination, and that's fine. Or you may find yourself fantasizing about sex a lot of the time. That's okay too. Some people go overboard with fantasies and find they cannot function sexually unless they act out a fantasy. That can be inconvenient, or may even become a problem for which professional help should be sought. That would depend on how the individual feels about the situation. In any case, having some fun with fantasies will not make you dependent on them.

Now some things for you to try:

> Spend some time relaxing with your eyes closed, thinking about the sexual fantasies that seem to be most common for you.

> If you don't have any fantasies that stick with you, try generating some. Look through some pictures or read some paragraphs that turn you on. Listen to sexy music or go to a movie. Then turn your imagination loose and see what fantasies you can invent. If they start getting unpleasant, you have the capability of moving on to something more positive.

> If you felt the exercises in this chapter, under "Step 3—your body responds," were sort of boring, try repeating them while fantasizing. Use pictures or reading materials if that helps. You might be surprised at how fantasy can expand your sexual enjoyment.

Step 5—keeping inner muscles in shape

Aside from basic cleanliness, the penis and testes require very little care. There are a few infections and other problems that may affect the male (see Chapter 6), but these difficulties are relatively rare. General physical health and condition have their effect on a man's energy level and therefore indirectly affect the amount of energy and stamina available for sex. For the most part, however, if a man is reasonably healthy, his sex organs will be able to function without a hitch. That doesn't mean that physical health will prevent certain psychological blocks from getting in the way. These are discussed in Chapters 4 through 6.

The penis is a pretty healthy organ. It gets a good blood supply, doesn't shrink with age, and has frequent erections. The testes just keep on making male hormones and hundreds of millions of sperm cells each day. Getting hit in the scrotum can be pretty painful, but even that usually doesn't do any harm. Even if by required surgery or some freak accident the testes are removed, the penis can go right on having erections and providing sexual pleasure.

There is one special exercise that I along with many professionals feel can help men maintain good internal sexual muscle tone. Only too often, men pay plenty of attention to the muscles that show so they can maintain external physical attractiveness, yet they ignore the internal musculature that may be so important to their own sexual pleasure. This special exercise involves contracting and relaxing the muscles that help to control ejaculation. It strengthens these muscles and helps assure good strong, satisfying orgasms. It may also provide a mild massage for the prostate gland (see pages 163–165) and keep that organ in healthy condition. Having the internal muscles in good shape gives men better control over their ejaculations, which can be important in preventing premature ejaculation (see Chapter 4).

Here is how to do this exercise, which contracts the *pubococcygeal* or *PC muscle*:

1. First you have to find the PC muscle. The simplest way is to stop your flow of urine while urinating. The muscle that you must contract to do this is the PC muscle. Also try tightening your anal opening, which is done with a closely related muscle. Next time you have an ejaculation during sex, notice that it is the same muscle that is involved in these contractions. You can feel the muscle getting very tense just prior to orgasm.

2. After you are familiar with the muscle, you will find it easy to contract it on your own. Try it. Make sure that no other part of your body moves. You don't have to squint, or suck in your stomach, or clench your fists, or move anything that will be visible to others. You can do this exercise anytime, anywhere, and no one will know it but you.

3. Now, make up your mind to do these PC muscle exercises regularly, fifty to one hundred times each day. Each con-

traction should be held for about six seconds. I usually recommend doing ten contractions at a time, five to ten times during the day. It's a good idea to do them at the same times each day. For example, you could do a "set" of ten contractions while shaving, another set while cleaning your teeth, another at lunch, and so on. If you have several telephone calls a day, you might do a set after each call.

4. After doing the exercises regularly for a few weeks, see if you can detect a difference in the strength and pleasurability of your ejaculations. Even if you don't notice a difference right away, the exercises will keep you in good shape for later life.

Aside from exercising the PC muscle, there is not a whole lot to keeping in good sexual shape. Regular physical exercise can keep you fit and develop stamina, both of which can contribute to good sex. Being constantly fatigued and out of shape doesn't make for the most active sex life, and yet many men get along fine with only minimal physical fitness.

What to expect from sex as you grow older

You probably have heard the jokes about old men who continue to chase women, but when they catch one, discover they've forgotten what they were chasing her for. There is a widespread attitude that aging means drying up sexually. Plenty of men are scared of getting old for just that reason. They see a loss of the sexual kick that has always meant so much to them.

Don, a construction foreman, hit his fiftieth birthday, and his spirits suddenly sagged. A friend of Don's, who was an acquaintance of mine, told me that he finally asked Don what was eating at him. Don had explained that he had just realized he was half a century old and that more than half his life was over. But more important, he had said, "Before long, I won't even be able to get it up anymore." The sad part of his situation is that if he goes on really believing that myth, it will probably come true (see Chapter 5). Don's fears are not unusual, nor are the possible effects of those fears.

In our society we have come to see aging as a process to be feared and fought. There is also an attitude that not only do older people lose their sexual needs and abilities, but they *shouldn't* have such feelings anyway. Many people are offended or disgusted by an old man or woman who still seems interested in sex. Some nursing homes and "old folks' " homes go to great lengths to see that their residents don't have the privacy for masturbation or other sexual outlets.

So what will be the effects of aging on your sex life as a male? There are two things for you to consider: your general physical health and your present level of sexual activity. Obviously, maintaining your health is important to feeling good no matter what your age. As you get older, it becomes increasingly important to eat properly without overindulging, get some regular physical exercise, avoid substances that are harmful (such as tobacco and excessive amounts of alcohol), take care of any ailments or physical problems that develop, not let yourself get overweight, and get a proper amount of rest. Sometimes, health problems develop that we have to learn how to live with, such as arthritis or heart trouble, but even people with serious illnesses can often find the energy and time for sex. In fact, for the reasonably healthy individual, sexual activity seems to be a good form of total body exercise.

Your present level of sexual activity may also give you some clues as to what to expect from your sexual future. The saying "Either use it or lose it" applies to sex to some degree. People who tend to put a low priority on sex during their youth and middle age will usually continue to give it low priority—or *no* priority—in their later years. There really is nothing wrong with that, and these people don't worry much about it. It's also generally true that people who are sexually active through middle age *can* continue having sex even into very old age. Even those who have been relatively inactive do not lose their ability to function sexually. If later on sex takes a higher priority in their lives—even if they are in their seventies, eighties, or older—a little practice can restore good functioning.

So don't despair. Old age does not mean an end to good sex. But let's be realistic too. Aging does slow you down to some extent. For one thing, your need for getting turned on and having orgasms gradually decreases, so you just don't have sex quite so often. Before you assume that this is depressing news, remember that the process is very gradual and that you adjust to it gradually. You don't wake up one morning full of the sexual desire of your youth but unable to do anything about it. It isn't a matter of being constantly frustrated. In fact, some older people are relieved not to feel quite so interested in sex. You will have to adjust in the way that is best for you.

Aging does have some predictable effects on the responses of your sex organs that men can easily learn to accept. They show up as you reach your later sixties and after, although they could be noticeable before then. For one thing, it will take you a bit longer to get a full erection as you age, and it may take a little extra work some of the time to keep an erection. You may notice that when you do have an erection, your penis doesn't stand out from your body at quite the same angle as when you were young, but a little lower. These are very gradual changes and they have no effect on the functioning of the penis.

As you get older, it may also take longer for you to have an orgasm once you've got an erection. For most men, this is not a disadvantage at all and instead makes for longer and more pleasurable sexual experiences. You also may not have quite so strong a need to have an orgasm each time you have sex. Many older men feel satisfied in some sexual contacts without ejaculating. This is hard for younger men to understand, since they often mistakenly assume that sex can't be fun or fully satisfying without ending in orgasm. When ejaculation does occur in old men, the semen doesn't spurt from the penis with the same force as it does in younger ones. It's more likely to ooze out of the penis. Nevertheless, the orgasm is pleasurable and relaxing.

Most everyone understands that after an orgasm it takes

longer for an older man to get aroused again. We all know of those times in life when you can have two orgasms—maybe even three—within a relatively short time. An older man usually can't do that, but the one orgasm he has, regardless of how seldom he has it, is plenty satisfying.

All in all, it's safe to say that regardless of how old you get to be, you'll be able to enjoy good sex. It may even find a more special place in your life. As one seventy-eight-year-old man once told me, "I don't do it quite so often anymore, but when I do, the fireworks are just as bright."

4

Coming Sooner
but Enjoying It Less?
How to Slow Down

Three men I know share a common sexual problem. I met
Brock through his wife, Helen. Sitting in my office, she explained she just wasn't interested in sex anymore. She dreaded
the times when Brock wanted to have intercourse. Questioning
her further, I discovered that earlier in their marriage,
she had always been easily aroused sexually but rarely had an
orgasm during intercourse. As I asked her for more details, she described their typically brief sexual encounters.
She had usually enjoyed intercourse, but just as she would be
starting to get into it, Brock would ejaculate and be finished.
This would happen within two or three minutes after they had
started. She was always left very turned on and frustrated, yet
too embarrassed to ask for more stimulation from him. As might
be expected, she gradually lost interest in sex, until she finally
stopped getting turned on at all. So sex turned into a problem
for both of them.

I asked Brock to come in alone for a counseling session, and
he agreed. Gradually I explained to him that I believed his
wife's "problem" to be partly his. "I know I just don't turn her
on anymore," he blurted out, "and how could I? I guess I'm
not much of a man. It seems that I just can't hold on for long.

I just get in her and I come off. I've tried just about every-thing, but I can't help it."

Dan was a college student who sought me out to talk specifically about his sexual difficulty. He had pretty much stopped dating altogether, though he was lonely and wanted a close, lasting relationship with a woman. But he had found that after a few dates, he felt pressured to get into sex. So he would quickly pull back from the relationship and drift away from the woman. It wasn't that Dan didn't want sex. Instead, he had learned to fear it because each of the six or seven times he had attempted intercourse, he had ejaculated almost immediately after entering the vagina. Once he had come just as he was starting to enter. It left him feeling embarrassed and dejected, ready to give up completely on sex.

Jay, a teacher in his mid-twenties, is bisexual. He sometimes has sex with women and sometimes with men. Recognizing that he has a tendency to ejaculate rapidly, he gets prepared. He told me about the "bag of tricks" he adopted to help with the problem. Usually, when he knows he's going to be having sex with someone, he masturbates ahead of time so that he won't be turned on later quite so easily. Once he excused himself to go to the bathroom just as he and his partner were heading for the bedroom, so he could give himself an emergency hand job. He also carries a little aerosol spray of a mild anesthetic that he bought from a mail order sex gadget place. He sprays the liquid on the head of his penis "to dull the sensations." During sex, he has some favorite mind games to keep himself from getting too turned on too fast. He either tries to do some math problems in his head, or imagines getting a phone call telling him that his brother has died. But despite his efforts, he rarely lasts more than five minutes before ejaculating.

All of these men were having trouble with what is usually called *premature ejaculation* or *rapid ejaculation*. There isn't an easy way to define what that means, because what is "premature" or "rapid" for one person may be perfectly acceptable and enjoyable for another. I usually talk about this problem in terms of *lack of ejaculatory control*. How fast a man reaches orgasm really isn't the point. The important thing is whether or not he has the ability to control the moment when his orgasm takes place, so that both he and his partner can enjoy themselves fully. Sometimes they both may want to have a quick and intense sexual encounter. Other times, they might want to linger with sex, drawing the experience out for a long time.

Don't get the mistaken idea that being able to delay ejaculation is just for the partner's sake. Not at all. The longer a male stays turned on and holds off orgasm, the more of a kick it usually has for him. It can mean the difference between a quick rub that produces a little shudder of an orgasm, and a pleasurable overall experience that climaxes with a total body orgasm you can feel right down to your toes.

Ejaculatory control is relatively easy to learn, but like anything worth having, it takes a little work and a little practice.

The over-anxious orgasm

Part of the problem in slowing down orgasm is that ejaculation is basically a reflex controlled by the spinal cord. When the penis is stimulated, messages build up in the nervous system until the "gun is fired," and that really doesn't take very long. Luckily, though, the whole process is not as simple as the knee-jerk reflex. You *can* learn how to exert some control over the ejaculation reflex—how to slow it down, put it off, and enjoy it more.

Many men never realize that they don't have to be at the mercy of their reflex. Dan's history was typical. He had learned to masturbate quickly. He had two brothers and two sisters, and sex was seldom discussed in his family. Sharing a room with one brother meant that he seldom had much privacy. The bathroom was in heavy demand. All this added up to his having the attitude that masturbation was something to get over with as soon as possible.

His first attempts at intercourse simply reinforced his pattern of coming quickly. His very first encounter took place in his own bedroom, with the fear that someone might discover them at any moment. The second time was in the cramped quarters of a car at a drive-in. All of his later sexual contacts had taken place in his dorm room, with the pressure of trying to finish before his roommate returned. When you consider the circumstances and remember the intense sexual excitement of a guy's first encounters, it's easy to see how Dan's problem arose.

It is also likely that if Dan hadn't tried to get some help in his college years, he might have ended up like Brock, building the rapid ejaculation pattern into his entire sex life. Brock had also learned to masturbate quickly and his early experiences were hurried.

Not all men who have trouble controlling ejaculation have the same type of background. I've talked with some who can last as long as they want in masturbation but are so much more turned on by sharing sex with another person, they just can't hold back. This is especially true of their first contacts with a new sexual partner. It is always especially exciting—and a little more nervous—those first few times. For some men, the position of their bodies for sex may have something to do with the problem too. In intercourse, for example, some men don't have as much difficulty delaying ejaculation while on their backs as they do when they're on top. And being nervous, scared, depressed, or angry can always aggravate the problem. The trouble is, once a man has experienced a few disappointingly rapid orgasms, he may get worried about it and have more trouble relaxing the next time. This sets up a vicious circle that can last a lifetime. The suggestions later in this chapter may help to break such vicious circles.

The battle to slow down

The little tricks Jay developed to slow himself down are not at all unusual. Most men find their own ways to delay ejaculation. Usually, they try to distract themselves as they begin to near orgasm. They may bite their tongue or lip, pinch themselves, squeeze their hands into fists, clench their teeth, or try to think some very nonsexy thoughts to get their minds away from sex. Some men don't have much luck with these techniques and find that they simply speed things up. Then there are the mild anesthetic sprays and creams (containing benzocaine) meant to be applied to the head (glans) of the penis. The advertising implies that they deaden the ability of the skin to sense sexual stimulation and therefore help to hold back ejaculation. Although some men report success with an anesthetic spray or cream, I have a feeling it is more the result of their being convinced it is going to work than of some actual physical effect.

The unfortunate element that all of these methods have in common is that they emphasize either reducing sexual excitement or distracting oneself from feeling sexual sensations fully. Instead of being able to relax and enjoy the sexiness of his body, a man must constantly watch to prevent himself from reaching orgasm. It is this very kind of worry and tension that may make the problem worse.

Once, in a panel discussion on sexuality at a college campus, I was discussing the importance of men learning ejaculatory control. A professor who was also on the panel broke in to say that he thought entirely too much emphasis was placed on the "timing" of sex. He claimed that men shouldn't worry about how long they took to reach orgasm and should instead be concerned about how good their relationships with other people were. I told the audience that I certainly agreed that the quality of a relationship is highly important. But relationships can suffer because of disappointing sexual contacts, resulting from poor ejaculatory control. Those who want to enjoy sex more and make their relationships better would be wise to concern themselves with the timing of their ejaculations.

To develop better ejaculatory control, I recommend not that you distract yourself from your sexual arousal, but rather that you get more closely in touch with it. Then you can control it better. The methods are quite simple, but to make them a natural part of you requires dedicated effort and practice. I have suggested the methods to over a hundred men, and every one who has reported results back to me (as nearly all have) has said that the exercises have *improved* his ability to lengthen the amount of time he takes to reach orgasm. Better yet, these men report *enjoying* sex more.

The preliminaries

To develop better control over your ejaculatory reflex takes some preparation. Before proceeding with the remainder of this chapter, think how you feel about your *body*, your *pace of living*, your *relationship(s)*, and your *attitude toward sex*.

1. *Your body.* One of the things that is important in learning orgasmic control is being sensitive to your own body. Plenty of men just do not pay much attention to the messages their bodies are constantly giving them. So if you haven't already, I suggest you back up and go through the exercises in Chapter 3. These may help you get more in touch with your own body and its sexual responses.

2. *Your pace of living.* Are you always in a rush? Is your life always tied up with tension and that feeling of having to hurry or get ahead? Read through the following questions and decide whether you would answer each one with a *yes* (if it usually could be applied to you) or a *no* (if it does not generally apply to you):

YES	NO	
———	———	Do you like to compete and try to win?
———	———	Do you often find it difficult to relax after a busy day?
———	———	Do you feel impatient and restless whenever you have to wait in line somewhere?
———	———	Does it often seem as if you just don't have time to accomplish everything you want to do?
———	———	Has anyone ever told you that you eat or drink too fast?
———	———	Do you often do more than one thing at a time, such as eating and reading, or writing while talking on the phone?

YES	NO	
_____	_____	Do you get irritated by being interrupted when you are in the middle of some important task?
_____	_____	Do you always arrive on time for appointments?
_____	_____	Do you tend to have a short temper?
_____	_____	Do you sometimes feel trapped by having many things to do?
_____	_____	Do you often have difficulty sleeping because of having many things on your mind?
_____	_____	Do you worry about whether or not you'll be promoted in your job?
_____	_____	Have you sometimes worked more than one job at a time to earn more money?
_____	_____	Have you neglected to take your full vacation time in recent years?
_____	_____	Do other people see you as someone who has a lot of energy?

If you have answered more than eight of these questions with a *yes*, you probably live at a stress-producing and hurried pace. Although this may have nothing to do with your sex life, I have discovered that some men who have difficulty with ejaculatory control are used to hurrying *everything*, including sex. If you want to, you probably can find ways of slowing down and taking more time for relaxation and fun.

3. *Your relationship(s).* Sometimes a crucial factor in controlling the amount of time to reach orgasm is the relationship you have with your partner. This may not seem to make much sense. After all, what should that have to do with how your penis works? The truth of the matter is that the way you feel about another person, and the kinds of things that are going on between you, really can affect your sexual functioning. You need to understand your tensions, games, and areas of poor communication. Any of these things may bring about too-rapid ejaculation. Communication will improve if you and your part-

ner work on things together. Some of the information and suggestions in Chapter 2 may help you with this. Or you may prefer to sit down with a third person and try to hash out difficulties. This is where counseling or sex therapy may be of help.

4. *Your attitude toward sex.* A lot of men think of sex as one continuous "operation," starting with the stimulation that leads to a buildup of sexual tension. The way these men see it, that tension just keeps rising without interruption until the peak is reached and orgasm happens. Sex doesn't have to be that way. There can be many peaks, and you don't have to go to the top of one of them until you're ready. That's really what the rest of this chapter is all about. A client of mine has expressed his prolonged enjoyment this way: "Why hurry with something that feels so good? There is no trick to having an orgasm, but that's only part of the fun. I like to get really close to coming and then back off and enjoy it longer. Then when I finally do get ready to let go, it is really powerful. My ejaculation seems to last forever. Yet, if I just want a quickie, I can always do that too. To me, a part of being a man is being able to have some control over my sexual enjoyment."

For some men, the following exercises will be the full answer for developing ejaculatory control. For others, they will only represent a beginning. See what they can do for you.

PHASE ONE: DEVELOPING EJACULATORY CONTROL ON YOUR OWN

Many sex therapists believe that the only way for a man to work on ejaculatory control is with the help of his partner. The trouble is, not all men have a partner available, and some men's partners aren't interested in working on the problem with them. Other men would simply rather do things on their own. In my experience there are many things that a man can do *on his own* to begin developing better control over his orgasms. Even if you have an available and willing partner, I would suggest giving these exercises a try first. Phase Two provides suggestions for involving your partner in this whole process.

You will have to be the judge of how quickly or how slowly you go through these exercises. Take your time—that's the whole point. Depending on how much progress you make and how often you feel like working on this, you may complete Phase One in a few days, or it may require a few weeks. You may have been learning a pattern of rapid ejaculation for years, so don't expect it to change overnight.

Two important steps must be mastered in developing ejaculatory control: (1) learning to detect that inner "warning signal" that you are soon going to ejaculate, and (2) learning the method that best helps you to pull back from ejaculating while continuing to enjoy sex. Again, these exercises should be done in a relaxed, private setting without any worry of being interrupted. You may want to begin with some relaxation exercises, such as those found on page 68.

Learning when to stop

The first step involves masturbating with your hand while lying on your back or propped up on pillows. Your body should be in a comfortable position. For this first exercise, do *not* use any lubricant on your penis or view any pictures. Just pay close attention to the feelings inside your body.

Stroke your penis slowly, grasping it as you usually do. Allow yourself to get a good full erection and try not to speed up your stroking too much as you get more excited. Take your time. As you are masturbating, notice how those inner muscles that help control ejaculation contract once in a while. It feels like a pleasurable fluttering. Keep masturbating, and you will gradually feel more and more tension building up in your entire body. You will begin to feel that desire to have an orgasm, and you know how good that feels. But keep in mind that delaying ejaculation can often make it even better.

As soon as you feel the tickling sensation that means orgasm is near—STOP. Just hold your penis loosely, but *do not move* your hand. Lie there and breathe deeply for a few moments. Almost immediately, the orgasm-warning feeling will go away. Do not start masturbating again until you are certain that you will not ejaculate right away. Then start again, moving your hand slowly until the warning signal returns, and then STOP again. See if you can bring yourself to this point *four times* without ejaculating. Try to draw the experience out longer than it would typically take you to masturbate—ten minutes or even longer. Nobody wants to judge sex by the clock, but during this learning process, using a clock can help you measure your progress. The fifth time, go ahead and ejaculate and let yourself enjoy it fully.

This is the *Stop-Start Method*, and it seems to work well for most men who try it. It allows you to enjoy sexual feelings, and you can simply slow down or stop the stimulation instead of ejaculating. If at any point you make a mistake and go a little too far past the first warning, you may reach the "point of no return" and have to ejaculate. Don't despair. You've learned a little more about your limits, so next time you can stop just that much sooner. Don't view a too-rapid ejaculation as a failure; you're still learning. Some men have success using a couple of other methods, the descriptions of which follow.

The squeeze—variation 1

The *Squeeze Method* is another simple technique that you can use on your penis at the moment you feel the inner warning of ejaculation. You might want to experiment with it to discover if it is more effective for you than simply stopping manipulation. When the warning signal begins to flicker, simply squeeze the head of your penis, with your thumb on the underside (frenulum) and your first and second fingers on the ridge around the top of the glans. Give yourself a good firm squeeze and hold it for four or five seconds. This will cause the feeling that you are about to ejaculate to go away. Your penis is not easily hurt when it is erect, so there shouldn't be any pain. You may lose some of your erection after the squeeze, but this should return easily once you begin masturbating again. After trying it a few times, if you decide you like the squeeze along with stop-start, I would again suggest squeezing yourself four times before finally allowing yourself to ejaculate.

There are some other ways of squeezing the penis that some men find effective. You can squeeze it around the base or middle of the shaft, for example, and often get the same result as squeezing the head. Experiment with different squeezes. My only objection to using the squeeze is that it is a little uncomfortable. In that sense it is similar to pinching yourself or biting your tongue, although it doesn't hurt the same way. In any case, some males like the squeeze and find that it works for them.

Bearing down—variation 2

The last chapter described exercises for keeping the pubococcygeal (PC) muscle in good tone. This muscle is involved in the inner contractions that produce ejaculation of semen. If you have been paying attention to your inner body sensations during sexual arousal, you have probably noticed that the PC muscle gets especially tense just before you have an orgasm. It is now believed that the tension of this muscle plays an important part in triggering ejaculation. Therefore, if you can learn how to relax the PC muscle in a hurry, you can delay orgasm.

There is a simple way to relax the PC muscle. In medicine, it is called a Valsalva maneuver, although I usually just call it *Bearing Down*. You act is if you are exhaling air from your lungs but close off the opening (glottis) at the base of your throat so that the air can't actually get out. It is exactly the same maneuver that you make when lifting something heavy or straining to push something. It relaxes your anal opening and the PC muscle. Try it and you will be able to feel what I am talking about.

Try using this bearing-down maneuver when you feel the inner warning signal of ejaculation. At first, anyway, you should use it with the stop-start method, at the same moment you stop. If it seems to work well for you, and you get used to using it, you may be able to bear down and have the ejaculatory feeling go away without completely having to stop stimulating your penis. But that takes practice, so don't expect miracles at first.

Continuing to experiment

So far this chapter has suggested that masturbating will help you identify the warning signal of ejaculation and has described three possible ways to prevent ejaculation: by stopping the stimulation soon enough, by squeezing your penis, or by bearing down with a Valsalva maneuver.

I recommend that you experiment with these new methods for *a minimum of five more times*. Each time, while lying or reclining on your back, masturbate to a point just prior to orgasm at least four times and ejaculate on the fifth. Continue using a clock to see how long you can prolong the experience. If you want to get to the warning signal more than five times without ejaculating, try it.

Also experiment with other ways of masturbating. Most of us get used to holding and stroking the penis in a particular way and always use the same approach. You may find that there are other grips or strokes that can help you last longer. For example, you might try holding the penis more loosely, or more tightly; using just two or three fingers or your entire hand; stroking only the shaft or just pulling at the glans; trying shorter strokes, and so on. Find the kinds of stimulation that help you last longest.

Gaining confidence

After you have made several tries at prolonging masturbation while lying on your back and without any lubrication, you should begin to feel that you are gaining more control over the moment when you ejaculate. Then move on to the next steps. Do not move on until you really feel that you have made progress, which will take some men longer than others.

Here are two exercises that can carry your control even further and help you to gain more confidence:

1. *Using a lubricant.* For most males, using some slippery lubricant on the penis during masturbation makes the experience even more sexy and pleasurable. At the same time the lubricant may make it even harder to slow down and delay orgasm. That is why using a lubricant is a good way to continue the exercise. Use whatever lubricant you like on your hand and penis. Some men like petroleum jelly (such as Vaseline), although this is more messy than K-Y jelly, mineral oil, body lotions, or massage oils and does not wash off easily. Soap and water are okay although you will have to keep adding a little water. Lotions and soap, if they get into the urethra, can cause some temporary—but painful—irritation, so be cautious. You may want to experiment to find the lubricant that provides the most pleasurable feeling for you.

Repeat the earlier exercises of slow masturbation using whatever technique you have found best when you feel the ejaculatory warning signal. You should still do this while lying down or reclining on your back. You will want to take your time at first, since the lubricant may heighten all of your sexual sensations, and you may want to come very quickly. Again, bring yourself close to orgasm, *without actually ejaculating*, at least four times before climaxing. You will probably want to repeat the exercise using the lubricant about six times over a period of several days. Watch the clock each time to see how long you take to reach orgasm.

Some men dislike using a lubricant. They either don't appreciate the "mess," find the sensations unpleasant, or just are too turned on by it to control their ejaculations. If you decide the lubricant is not adding anything to the experience, discontinue it. However, if you dislike it because it is so stimulating and makes you come faster, I would suggest sticking with it and this exercise until you finally get some confidence in your ability to slow down.

2. *Using fantasy and pictures.* In the last chapter I dis-

cussed how sexy fantasies, pictures, books, and movies may expand your sexual enjoyment. The next stage of gaining confidence in your ability to control your ejaculations involves getting yourself turned on with the fantasies, pictures, or other materials that really get you revved up. Use your turn-on materials while masturbating, also using a lubricant. Use the same method as before to delay orgasm—whichever works best for you.

Shifting positions

Up until now, all of these exercises have been done in the most relaxed position possible, lying down or reclining. Yet many sexual activities are done standing up, or on your side, or kneeling, or prone. For some males these other positions create the sort of inner muscular tension that hurries them to orgasm. So now you can try some other positions for masturbation.

With all of your clothes removed, apply a lubricant to your hand (or both hands if you want) and your penis. Have your favorite fantasies or pictures there too. Then turn over so that you are lying face downward and put your penis in your hand(s). This time, instead of moving your hands, move your pelvis, slowly thrusting your penis in and out of the hands. At first, anyway, you may find it more difficult to maintain control in this position. But remember everything you have learned. You know how your inner warning signal feels; you know what method works for you to stop yourself from having an ejaculation; you know how long you can delay having the ejaculation. You can do all the same things in this position too. Again, do not have an orgasm until at least the fifth time of getting close to it. And then you should repeat the entire exercise several times over a period of days, until you feel really confident in your ability to control your ejaculation.

You may want to experiment with a variety of other positions, just to find out how well you can control yourself in different situations. Use any position that would be typical of some sexual activity you might share with a partner. Experiment to develop your confidence.

These exercises have helped a good many men develop better ejaculatory control on their own. You can use them whether or not you have a regular sexual partner. What you learn on your own will serve you well when and if you are with a partner for sex. It is usually wise, however, to involve a partner whenever possible in helping you develop ejaculatory control. It can be fun to work together on this process, and it certainly can improve your sex life together unless your partner likes to have things over with in a hurry.

PHASE TWO: DEVELOPING EJACULATORY CONTROL WITH A COOPERATIVE PARTNER

Nearly all of the men with whom I have worked have had no trouble transferring what they have learned on their own to their sexual relationship with a partner. Hamilton was an exception, however. He had done all the steps faithfully on his own and had gained plenty of confidence in his ability to delay ejaculation. He had reached the point where he could keep masturbating indefinitely without having an orgasm until he wanted to. He felt good about that, and he was ready to start working his new control into his sexual contacts with women. The day after his first attempt at doing so, he entered my office with a glum face. "I couldn't even last a minute," he said sadly. "I don't understand what went wrong."

As I questioned Ham further about the experience, I found out that he and his partner had spent a long time in heated foreplay, including oral sex. He had come close to ejaculating several times but was able to hold back. Anyway, by the time he started having intercourse, he was very close to orgasm. Ham had also not bothered to tell her that he was working on developing better ejaculatory control, and she had continued to assume that he wanted her to stimulate him as heavily and rapidly as before. As we talked it all over, Ham admitted that this had made him angry and that he had almost felt as if she were spoiling everything. When he had come so rapidly, she had obviously been disappointed and a little angry herself, and that only increased Ham's own feelings of failure. All in all, everything had worked against this being a good, lasting sexual contact for both of them.

Basic approaches with a partner

When trying to have good ejaculatory control with a partner, you should keep several things in mind that Hamilton didn't:

Partners aren't mind readers. If your partner is going to help you develop your ejaculatory control, you have to let your partner know what to do. That means that you will need to have a pretty good idea what you want from your partner and then care enough about the two of you to communicate it.

Talking it over with your partner. To work on this together, both of you should feel free to exchange your thoughts, feelings, and needs openly. You are bound to feel some embarrassment, worry, and tension about this whole process. Your partner may have some concerns about it too. It will be important that both of you be able to share these feelings and ideas and work on them together. Be sure you have read Chapter 2.

Your partner will need to be understanding. You will have to let your partner know that being understood is important to you. Ham's partner felt cheated by his coming too fast, and that made her angry and resentful. Maybe if she had known how important the whole thing was to him, she could have been more understanding and supportive. But again, you will have to let your partner know what you need in the way of understanding.

When you do ejaculate too soon, it doesn't have to be viewed as a "failure." Just about every male comes sooner than he wants once in a while. The worst thing to do is to panic. That will simply make you more tense and anxious next time, and you'll just ejaculate that much sooner. Instead, whenever you do come too soon, learn from it. Think about why it happened and how it could have been prevented. Talk over feelings with your partner. Maybe you can even have a good laugh over it.

Don't ignore "messages from your penis." Sometimes, ejaculating too soon represents a message from your penis that you just weren't listening to. Your penis may be saying something to you like "Let's get this over with and get out of here." Or "You're angry with her so let's punish her by finishing off too soon." Or "You don't really want to be doing this so hurry up." These are the kinds of messages that may mean that the problem lies more in the quality of the relationship than in how well you have learned ejaculatory control. Counseling or therapy from a qualified professional may be necessary at these times. See Chapter 7.

If your relationship is a relatively close one, and you keep these approaches in mind, you will probably have good luck working together on developing your ejaculatory control. The remainder of the chapter gives you exercises to help things along.

Enjoying each other's bodies

A good start for working on ejaculatory control is getting relaxed with each other's bodies. Before you get into anything really sexual, try this exercise a few times.

Both of you should remove all of your clothing and, if you both enjoy it, undress each other slowly. If you're not used to doing this, it may seem a little silly or embarrassing, so if you feel like laughing, just be careful not to laugh *at*, only *with*.

You might also want to bathe or shower together, soaping each other's backs, washing each other's hair, and so on. Dry each other off when you finish. Relax together and have a good time. The one rule for this entire exercise is that *neither* of you should touch the other's sex organs. You are not going to end up doing anything sexually. I just want you to relax and enjoy your bodies together.

In a warm, comfortable, and private place, dim the lights if you wish and put on some relaxing music. Then take turns touching and massaging each other. Remember: *avoid the sex organs*. Make a special effort to be gentle and caring, as you trace, stroke, and massage fingers and hands over the other's body. The one being touched need only relax and fully enjoy all of the pleasant sensations. If you find a particular way of being touched unpleasant, suggest that your partner try something a little different. Avoid such strong negative messages as "Don't do that," or "I don't like it that way." Instead, say something positive, like "How about a little lighter touch there, and maybe a circular motion." As you're being touched, don't let your mind be charged with thoughts about how you are going to "pay" the other person back or other worries. Be selfish and enjoy all the attention you're getting. When it is your turn to touch your partner, simply do what feels good and right to you and take whatever suggestions your partner offers.

Both of you may get sexually aroused by all of this touching, and that is fine. But it is also okay not to get turned on. Sexual arousal is not the goal of this exercise. If you do get aroused, be sure *not* to have sex together right then. That shouldn't happen until after you've worked on other exercises later. The next exercises are aimed at developing further confidence in your ability to control your ejaculations.

You may do the mutual touching for as long as you both find it pleasurable. I suggest a minimum of twenty minutes for the entire exercise—ten minutes for each of you to be touched. I also suggest that you do the exercise a *minimum of two times* over a period of at least two days, before progressing to the next stage. You may want to spend several days with the mutual body pleasuring, depending on how long it takes for both of you to feel really relaxed and comfortable with one another. Remember to talk over any tensions, embarrassments, and other feelings that come up, including the good ones.

Light sexual stimulation

By doing the last exercise, the two of you could relax together and not have sexual satisfaction as your goal. This next exercise is an intermediate step, designed to stimulate your sex organs and your partner's lightly, but not intended to generate intense sexual arousal or orgasm. This time the two of you should relax and enjoy whatever sexual feelings you have, but not worry about carrying through to orgasm.

Basically, get prepared in the same way you did for the last exercise and start with some stroking and massaging over the entire body. Take turns giving and getting the touching. This time, however, feel free to touch each other's sexual organs. Don't jump in with rubbing or any intensive sex play. Just use some light teasing of the sex organs and surrounding area— gentle touches and light caresses. Many people get quite aroused by this sort of stimulation, but not everybody. Again, you should not share sex yet. I suggest doing this exercise at least *twice* before moving to the next stage. If you begin to get so turned on that you want to have sex, stop and get out of bed. If you decide that you absolutely can't wait, then at least do what the next set of exercises suggests.

Stop-start stimulation by partner

This is where you and your partner are going to begin working specifically on developing your ejaculatory control. The principles are basically the same as the masturbation exercises described earlier, except this time your partner is going to be providing the stimulation. Ask your partner to read through all of the exercises described in Phase One, pages 91–98 in this chapter, and explain what techniques you have found most useful in delaying ejaculation. Then proceed with the exercises together.

Stop-start: stage 1. While you lie nude on your back in a comfortable position, your partner should either straddle your legs while facing you or sit beside you to have easy access to your penis. Work out a signal between you so that you can easily let your partner know when you feel that you are about to ejaculate. Simply saying "stop" might work fine. Have your partner begin by slowly, gently stimulating your penis with a dry hand. This stimulation should continue until you feel your inner ejaculatory warning signal. Immediately signal for the partner to stop stimulating you. Use the bearing-down method if you find it helpful. If you have found the squeeze method effective, then teach your partner how to squeeze your penis in the way that works best. All you have to do in this exercise is to lie back and enjoy yourself. Just be certain to signal in time so you don't ejaculate before you mean to.

Just as you did on your own, have your partner bring you close to orgasm at least four times before actually ejaculating. Do this exercise over a period of days until you both feel confident that you can control when you ejaculate. If your partner wants to be able to have some sexual enjoyment too, then work out a way to stimulate her or him without involving your penis. That will happen later.

Stop-start: stage 2. When you both feel ready, repeat the stimulation of the penis while you are still lying on your back. This time, your partner should use lubrication on the hand or mouth stimulation, whichever you both enjoy and find most enjoyable. The stimulation should be slow and controlled. Offer any suggestions to your partner that would be of help to you. Again, signal so that stimulation can be stopped before you ejaculate and apply whatever method works best for you. Carry the whole sequence through and keep up with the exercise until you're ready to move on.

Stop-start: stage 3. When you feel confident in your ability to control your orgasms, you may move on to the kind of sexual act that used to lead to premature ejaculation. That might be intercourse, oral sex, or any other activity involving your penis. If possible, begin while lying on your back. Here are some further suggestions:

If you are going to have vaginal intercourse with a woman, then start out with her straddling you. As soon as you have a firm erection, she can crouch over your penis and slip it into her vagina. By now, she will be aware that she must move slowly as she slides her body up and down on the penis. You may want to do some cautious thrusting yourself, but don't get carried away. Again, use your signal whenever you feel that you are about to ejaculate. Then she can immediately stop moving. If necessary, she can also move off your penis right away and apply the squeeze. Whatever method you use, you will feel the inner warning go away, and then you can start in again. Repeat this until you have come close to orgasm and have stopped at least four times. Then, when you are both ready, go ahead and ejaculate, fully enjoying your stored-up "kick." It will take some practice to get this whole process really working for the two of you, so if you happen to ejaculate a little too soon, don't be upset. You will be able to be more careful next time.

As you feel more confident, you will gradually be able to move into other positions. Try having intercourse while you both are on your sides before moving into the position where you are on top. Every step of the way, use the signal to your partner whenever necessary. It won't be long at all before you can control your own movements so that you can stop and start as you want. Remember that the bearing-down Valsalva maneuver can be used any time to help.

If you are working toward having more ejaculatory control in some sexual activity other than intercourse, the principles are still the same. Start while you are on your back and signal your partner to stop as necessary. Gradually work together so that you can move into whatever positions you both prefer.

Sexual self-reliance

If you tend not to have as much control over your ejaculations as you would like, *you* can do something about it. *You* can gain confidence in your sexual control and end up having much more enjoyable sexual experiences—alone and with someone else.

Remember Dan, the college student from the beginning of this chapter? Dan had good success with Phase One of developing ejaculatory control. He reported to me that in his masturbation he could last about as long as he wanted. Usually he tried to take about fifteen or twenty minutes with stimulation before ejaculating. He was feeling very confident with himself. Eventually, he started dating again and developed a close relationship with Sally. This time, though, he took his time with the relationship and developed good lines of communication. As they gradually began to get involved sexually, Dan was able to explain to Sally about his sexual concerns and how he had been working to develop more ejaculatory control. Sally told him that she would really enjoy working with him on developing the control.

I talked with Dan and Sally together just before they started Phase Two. The whole program went along quite rapidly for them, probably because they had already developed good lines of communication about sex. They stopped by a couple of times as they were working together just to let me know about their progress. I simply told them that things seemed to be going well.

Using the relatively simple techniques described in this chapter, Dan and Sally were able to develop an excellent sexual relationship in which Dan was able to last as long as either of them wanted him to. Sally always had an orgasm, sometimes two or three. Best of all, they both felt as if they were taking responsibility for their own sexual enjoyment. They had chosen to work together to make an important part of their relationship as good as possible. They were proud of that, and the whole process had brought them closer together.

Even though Brock and Jay had been troubled by lack of ejaculatory control for a longer period of their lives, these training techniques also worked rapidly for them. Brock was able to stop blaming his wife and squarely face the responsibility he needed to take for slowing down during sex. Jay gradually learned how to enjoy his sexual responses without having to invent ways of distracting himself. All of these men had learned what self-reliance in sex can mean.

5

---◆---

Going Limp–
What to Do about
Impotence

The sexual problem men dread and fear the most is impotence. The first thing to do to get a better perspective on it is to stop calling it *impotence*, because that word magnifies the difficulty all out of proportion. Impotence is failure and weakness; it means that a man is without force, lacking in strength and power—all because his penis doesn't get as erect as he thinks it should or would like it to. No wonder so many men who think of themselves as "impotent" feel so depressed and helpless.

The male failure trap also extends into areas of life other than sex. Most men seem to expect that they will succeed at everything they try, an unrealistic hope at best. So when something doesn't go as they expected, or they fail at some single task in their lives, they magnify it into "I am a failure." How much better it would be if we could say things to ourselves such as "I'm not very good at golf" or "This job didn't work out for me" or "I wasn't a very sensitive father last night," instead of turning those unmet expectations and dreams into a massive, frightening, clutching sense of *total failure*. There are always more parts of our lives where we can see strength and success if we want to bother looking for them.

Likewise, it is unrealistic to expect that our every sexual encounter will be a fully successful, fully satisfying, and enjoyable experience. As with everything else in life, sex has its ups and downs. The trouble is, when his penis is down and he wants it up, the average man panics. He finds it difficult to say to himself or his partner something like "Well, I guess this just isn't the time; maybe next time." There is always the pressure to succeed—right now, right here.

Instead of calling it impotence, I want to call it what it is: not having an erection. It is important for men and women to understand that all three stages of sexual response: desire, tension building, and tension releasing—are easily influenced by emotions, fatigue, and anything else that affects our bodies. Erection of the penis is usually one of the signs by which men know that their bodies are responding to sexual stimulation. But erection can be easily influenced by many different distracting factors.

The vicious circle effect

One fact that most men don't realize is that when they are turned on sexually, the hardness of the penis may vary from minute to minute. It may be fully erect for a period of time, and then it may get softer for a while. That is a very normal part of male sexual arousal. However, if the male feels a pressure to succeed and panics when his penis happens to lose some of its erection, he is likely to generate inner anxiety and tension that will make it impossible, or at least difficult, to get his full erection back. This results in more tension, and he begins to fear that he has really lost the erection for good. That is the fear and anxiety that he will carry with him to his next sexual encounter, and it will set up the tense conditions for erection problems a second time. For some men this vicious circle just keeps going around and around, sometimes for months or years.

Charlie's situation was a good example of this vicious circle effect. He began having intercourse with a steady girl friend at the age of fifteen, and they continued this sexual relationship until he left home to attend a community college. After the first month at school, he met a woman whom he liked and after two dates they decided to go to bed together. They spent little time getting down to business, and when Charlie attempted to enter the woman's vagina, he ran into difficulty. Their sex organs were quite dry, and he had trouble finding the vaginal opening with his fingers. He found himself fumbling awkwardly to begin intercourse and suddenly noticed that he had lost much of his erection. Since this had never happened to him before, he was startled and embarrassed. After a few more minutes of useless fumbling, he rolled over and made up an excuse that he was too tired. Over the next few weeks they enjoyed a variety of other sexual activities together, and Charlie had no particular difficulty with erection except whenever they attempted intercourse. His partner was patient, but they never talked much about what was happening. Each time they would give up on intercourse and go back to other sex play. Over the next two years, this pattern continued with the three other women Charlie dated. By the time he came to my office, he was fully convinced that it was impossible for him to have intercourse, although some of the exercises in this chapter soon restored his confidence.

Charlie had been trapped into a vicious circle by allowing himself to be frightened by a simple, natural softening of his penis. He really locked the trap door when he failed to communicate with his partner about his feelings. His manhood script demanded that he never seem unsure of himself, especially in sex. Consequently, he kept all of his fear and embarrassment inside.

Erection of the penis is the part of male sexual responsiveness that is probably more immediately susceptible to emotional and physical stress than any other. It is largely an involuntary bodily reaction—you cannot will it, force it, or command it. But you do have to be relaxed enough, physically and emotionally, to let it happen.

But it never worked!

Josh, a senior in college, looked glum as he came into my office. He beat around the bush for several minutes before explaining how depressed he was that his two attempts at having sex with a new girl friend had been thwarted by erection problems. He said that he just didn't understand what was wrong with him. I began asking some questions that would help us get a clearer idea of what had prevented his penis from getting hard. He interrupted me by saying, "But it never worked. I've tried to have sex with every girl friend I've had since I was fourteen and haven't succeeded yet."

As we talked further, it became clear that Josh only had erectile difficulty when attempting intercourse. Everything worked fine during masturbation and petting. His penis just would not remain hard whenever he tried to get it into a vagina. Josh fit into the group of males who have never been able to succeed in keeping an erection long enough to finish whatever sexual activity they would like to have. A problem of such long duration is not as common as the erection difficulty that develops later in one's life after some successful experiences. However, there are still thousands upon thousands of men who have never managed to complete the sexual act they so desire. Many of them eventually give up in despair, not realizing that there are ways of improving their situation.

If you are having problems getting or keeping an erection, the approaches discussed later in this chapter may well help you, regardless of whether or not you have ever "succeeded" in sex before. Be sure you also read the earlier chapters in the book, especially Chapters 2 and 3. And try to have confidence. You can learn how to relax and enjoy sex like anyone else.

The myth that sex requires full erection

The male's penis is filled with nerve endings in its skin that make it especially sensitive to touch. Most forms of touch stimulation to the penis are pleasurable to men, whether or not the penis is erect. In other words, full erection is not necessary for penile stimulation to feel good and be enjoyable. Full erection is not even always necessary for intercourse or ejaculation to occur.

Our society places a great deal of emphasis on intercourse

as the best and most desirable form of sexual sharing. Actually, there is a host of other sexual activities that people may enjoy together, and most of them do not demand a hard-as-rock erection from the male. There are many body parts other than the penis that can provide sexual stimulation to a partner as well, ranging from your hair and tongue all the way down to your big toe. Any man who relies only on his penis to give himself or his partner pleasurable sexual sensations is selling the whole rest of his body short and setting himself up for some pretty dull, humdrum sex.

When for any reason a man has difficulty keeping his erection, his sexual pleasuring need not end. If more men understood this, there would be a lot fewer problems with erections.

Medical problems and erection

When a penis doesn't get as erect as its owner would like, there are usually emotional stresses that are getting in the way. However, erection also may be affected by physical stress, and a variety of illnesses and other medical problems may lead to erectile difficulties. Anytime a man is feeling sick or run-down because of some illness, his sexual responsiveness may be slowed down or even halted for a while.

Following a serious illness, such as a heart attack or stroke, many men are simply afraid to get turned on. They remember how their bodies used to get revved up during sex and fear that they are going to do themselves more damage. Unfortunately, many physicians neglect to talk with their patients about sexual activity following some serious malady, and many patients are too embarrassed to ask for more information. The fear and lack of information may lead to erection difficulties. Illness almost never means that a man's sex life must end (also see Chapter 6). Usually, after recovery is underway, it's a good idea to start a return to normal sexual life with nonstrenuous masturbation, for example, before attempting more taxing shared activities. The best policy is to check with your physician for advice on how far to go and how soon.

There are some physical conditions that may cause problems in achieving erection. Diabetes seems to be connected with erectile difficulties in some men, although if diabetic males keep their sugar levels properly regulated there are usually no lasting problems. Certain prostate infections and diseases of the nervous system may interfere with erection, but these are uncommon. Some physicians treat erectile problems by giving the man a male hormone, such as testosterone, either by pill or by injection. However, there is evidence to indicate that hormone treatment is ineffective unless tests have shown the man to have abnormally low levels of testosterone, also a rare disorder.

The message is clear, however. If you are having continuing erection problems, even during masturbation, and in addition if you notice that you no longer get erections during the night or upon waking, consult a physician. Often a urologist or physician specializing in sexual illnesses would be the best choice. However, investigate first. Not all physicians know much about erectile difficulty. If you don't seem to be getting anywhere after a reasonable length of time, try another doctor.

Hank had been troubled for several months by an inability to have a full erection, and he consulted his family doctor. After a routine physical exam, the doctor told Hank there was no physical basis for the problem and advised him to seek counseling. I had seen Hank for three sessions and had given him several sexual exercises to try at home before I began to think that the doctor might be wrong. He just wasn't responding to treatment. I also discovered that there were many cases of diabetes among the families of both his parents. So I referred Hank to another physician for further tests, and sure enough, an early stage of diabetes showed up. As soon as medical treatment was begun, his erectile problems disappeared.

Alcohol and erection
Many people find that alcohol relaxes them and loosens them up. They may find it easier to get sexually involved after some

drinks. However, alcohol is a substance that slows down the activity of the central nervous system, having a *depressant* effect. Beyond a certain level of concentration in the body, which varies in different individuals, alcohol can slow down sexual response and lead to difficulty in getting an erection. For the average drinker, this effect is temporary, but for some men the temporary erection problem triggers a fear of "failure" that sets up a continuing vicious circle. Heavy drinkers sometimes completely lose the ability to sustain a full erection for their sexual activities.

Ellis had a pattern in his life of meeting women in singles bars and then having sex with them. He was convinced that the best way to get really turned on was to start with a few drinks, let your barriers down, and let loose. It worked for him for over three years. During that period he gradually increased the number of drinks he would have on a typical night out. He began to notice that it was taking him longer to get a fully erect penis, but since he was also lasting longer during sex, that didn't really matter to him. One night, however, he was alarmed to be unable to keep an erection long enough to have intercourse for more than a few seconds at a time. He kept trying until he was worn out and finally gave up. That time he wrote it off to fatigue, but when it happened again the next five times he attempted sex, he decided to seek help. I worked with Ellis for several weeks to reduce his drinking habit and to help him regain his ability to sustain an erection. His situation was a good example of a person who became a problem drinker without ever realizing it until his sex life was affected. Most sex therapists seem to agree that in the long run, heavy drinking and sex just don't mix.

Any depressant or tranquilizing drug can cause erection problems. Smoking marijuana seems to heighten sexual feelings for some people, but heavy use may interfere with erection in a few men. Again, anything that affects our mood or our body's responses may have an effect on erection of the penis. If you are experiencing any difficulty with erection, check if the use of alcohol or any kind of medication or drug might be a possible cause.

Erection as a barometer

When Kurt came to my office for the first time, he seemed bewildered and depressed. "About two months ago," he explained, "I was impotent for the first time in my life. I thought it was just one of those things, but it has kept happening. Since then I've been able to have intercourse with my wife only once. Every other time we try, I just can't seem to get it up." As we explored the problem together, it was evident that there were no medical problems. Kurt was able to masturbate with a full erection; it was just when he attempted intercourse with his wife that his penis went limp.

Kurt gradually told me a story that helped explain his situation, although it took him a long time to realize fully how his marital relationship was contributing to his lack of erection. He and his wife had been married for four years, and he admitted that he had always seen her as the "stronger" of the two. He was usually the one to decide that he wanted to have sex. Often, she would either refuse or grumble that she wasn't much in the mood.

Their communication patterns were poor. They both apparently had stored up plenty of anger and resentment against each other over past hurts. They argued frequently, and their arguments only created more tension rather than resolving conflicts. They rarely talked about sex either, and their bedroom contacts had become routine and mechanical. As Kurt and I talked, his negative feelings toward his wife began to emerge. He was angry with her and somewhat afraid of her temper. He found her moods unpredictable and often felt as if he actually disliked her. It was not really very surprising that his penis was not rising to attention whenever he thought it should.

It took several weeks for Kurt and his wife to take a closer look at what was happening in their relationship. When they realized what was going on, they both decided to work on the problems together to save their entire relationship. It took plenty of work too, and it meant facing some rough feelings, but they made it. The sexual exercises gradually led to improved sex, and Kurt began having erections again.

For many men, their penises are barometers of their emotional lives. When a man is relaxed, relatively happy, and together, his penis will get erect with appropriate stimulation. But if he is tense, depressed, or having some other unsettled feelings roiling under the surface, his penis may well register the situation for him by not rising. Some men seem fairly able to separate their emotions from their erections, but for many others, the rising and falling of their penises is a measure of what is going on inside.

TONY. Tony looked like a pro football player. He was thick and muscular. He didn't consult me about any sexual problems, but during our conversations about other matters he told me about some former trouble. Tony had always tried to live up to his macho image. He wanted to be tough, impersonal, brave, and able to have any woman he wanted. Most of the time he and the image succeeded—except in bed. There he could rarely get an erection. Now that he had fallen in love with a young woman and settled into a happy sex life with her, he was able to understand his earlier erection problems: "That macho thing just wasn't me. I was going to bed with anything that walked. I didn't care about them and they didn't care about me. Most of the time I wasn't even turned on by those women. I just assumed my prick would work anytime, anywhere, regardless of the circumstances. Now I realize that it was just being more honest than I was—neither of us really wanted to be there." It is surprising how many men try to live up to dishonest roles that do not fit them at all. But it is not very surprising that their penises sometimes won't cooperate with the masquerade.

WILL. Will's erection problems stemmed from other sexual disappointments that built up over a period of years. He had always experienced difficulty controlling his ejaculations. At first, none of his sexual partners complained, but he got a vague sense that he should be able to "last longer" during sex. Things really didn't hit home until he had been married for six months. His wife finally asked him if he could try to last longer during sex because she wasn't getting much enjoyment out of their brief encounters. Nearly every time, though, Will would end up ejaculating before either of them wanted, and he would feel as if he had let his wife and himself down. He began to dread sex more and more, and their frequency of intercourse declined. Eventually, he even stopped getting erections. Will's case was not at all unusual. Males who find sex unrewarding and lacking in fun because of some continuing sexual failure often get so tense about it that they cannot even respond with an erect penis.

TIM. This young man was not getting erections because he was attempting a sexual way of life that did not fit him— heterosexuality. He wanted very much to be "straight," mainly because he had the mistaken idea that every "normal" man should be turned on by women. Well, he was not and instead was sexually attracted to other men. Somehow, he believed that if he made it with enough women, he could not possibly be gay. His penis apparently knew better, since it rarely functioned the way he wanted when he attempted sex with a female. It took several weeks of counseling for Tim to begin accepting that being gay was not the end of the world and that he could find a happy and satisfying life. As a matter of fact, as soon as he became comfortable with the idea of loving other men, and he tried sex with some others of his own sex, his erection problems disappeared.

JEFF. Of all the men I have worked with in counseling and therapy, Jeff was the most convinced of his *impotence*. He worked for his father in a job that he hated. Yet he felt trapped by the expectation that he would naturally be the one eventually to take over the family business, which he also hated.

He had made some investments that had not paid off, although he had never dared admit this to his father. Every day he felt depressed and tired. It was little wonder that all of Jeff's feelings of powerlessness and failure expressed themselves in his constant inability to get an erection. His penis was simply reflecting the quality of his life—limp and flimsy. Eventually, however, Jeff began to realize his ability to make choices and decisions for himself. After he got a sense of his own inner strength and power, his penis also began responding to sexual arousal.

DICK. Dick had hit the age of sixty and decided that he was old. He also believed that old men didn't—and shouldn't—have sex. And so a man who had never experienced any sexual difficulties stopped having erections. This alarmed his wife, but Dick refused to talk about it. When the couple finally consulted a sex therapist, Dick's feelings about sex and aging began to emerge. With some more accurate information and some reassurance, he was soon functioning again during sex.

These brief case studies could go on and on because there are so many common causes of erectile difficulty. Guilt and fear are often at the root. If a man has something inside telling him that a sexual experience isn't right, or if he's scared of getting caught, or if he doesn't trust the method of birth control, he can go limp. A man who has a religious background or parental teaching that puts sex in a negative light may have difficulty responding with an erection. When the manhood script calls for topnotch sexual performance, the pressure may be sufficient to destroy his performance completely. Finally, any man who tries to get involved with another person sexually while tired out, drunk, or just not in the mood may be asking for trouble. Likewise, men have to be able to feel comfortable enough with communication so that they can let partners know which kinds of stimulation get the best results.

Regardless of the causes behind erection problems, most men can be helped to regain their erectile capabilities with some simple exercises. They are described in the remainder of this chapter. However, before you try them, take a closer look at yourself with the following questionnaires.

WHAT ABOUT YOU?

If you are presently experiencing some difficulty getting or maintaining an erection, or if you have worried about some difficulty in past experiences, the following two questionnaires may help you to understand what happened. The first will help you sort through some information from your past sexual development and your sexual attitudes, and the second will help you take a closer look at what was going on when your penis was not responding as you wished.

Looking back

Spend some time thinking about your answers to the following questions:

1. Did you have religious training earlier in your life that emphasized the immorality of various forms of sex, such as sex outside marriage? How much did these teachings mean to you, and how much do they mean now?

2. What sorts of messages did you get from your parents concerning sex? Did they help you to feel that sex was a positive and good thing, or did they give you a more negative attitude?

3. How did you feel about your body during your teenage years, and how have you felt about it during recent years and months?

4. Recall in as much detail as possible the first time you encountered any erection problems during sex. Whom were you with, and how did you feel about the other person? Try to remember how you were feeling about the sexual

contact, and how you reacted when your penis was not as hard as you wanted.

5. Have you always viewed a good firm erection as necessary to sex and as a sign of being a full man? If so, how did this attitude develop? Think about it.

When you go limp

This questionnaire can help you evaluate what may be going on when you actually have trouble getting an erection. In each section, check whichever statements apply to you. For every section in which you have made any checks, read the *suggested action* at the end. When you have finished the entire questionnaire, spend some time putting together an overall plan for dealing with erection problems, now or in the future.

Check any statements that apply to you.

_____ I have not had any erection problems in recent sexual encounters; my problems were in the past.

_____ Most of the time, I have a good erection. Once in a while, I have some trouble keeping an erection.

_____ I have been unable to complete a few sexual acts recently, although more often than not, I don't have any trouble.

Suggested Action: Don't worry. Most men experience erectile difficulties sometimes. Some sex therapists don't even see it as a problem worth treating unless it is occurring in more than 25% of attempts at sex. The important thing, always, is not to get involved in sex unless you really feel a desire to do so and have a partner with whom you feel comfortable. In any case, it is up to you to decide whether you are going limp often enough to consider it a problem. The exercises in this chapter may help you to improve the situation, regardless of whether or not it has to be a problem.

_____ I never get a full erection.

———— I have been feeling run-down and tired lately. That seems to make me uninterested in sex and makes it difficult to get an erection.

———— I am recovering from a major illness and have been afraid to exert myself too much in sex.

———— I used to get erections but now almost never do. I don't even notice erections when I awake from sleep.

———— I have noticed erection problems since taking a new medication.

———— I can't even get a full erection when I masturbate, nor during activity with a partner.

———— I have been having erection problems, and there is a history of diabetes in my family, or I am diabetic myself.

———— I have been having discomfort or bleeding during urination, bowel movements, or sex.

———— During sex I have pain elsewhere in my body that makes me lose my erection.

Suggested Action: See a physician and explain what has been going on. Before proceeding with any of the body exercises in this chapter, you should check out whether or not any medical problems exist that might be interfering with your erection responses. If physical causes are thoroughly ruled out, you may want to work through the chapter exercises or consult a professional sex therapist.

———— I notice erection problems after drinking alcohol.

———— I notice erection problems after using an unprescribed drug.

Suggested Action: Cut down on your consumption, or cut it out altogether, and see if there is any improvement in your erections. If there is none, you might want to consult a physician and/or begin working on the exercises in this chapter.

_____ My problems with erections began after an incident when I lost my erection with a partner and panicked.

_____ I have been trying to live up to an all-male image, and my penis sometimes doesn't cooperate.

_____ I had been having trouble with another sexual problem and eventually began to have erection problems.

_____ I seldom feel very turned on by the partners I attempt to have sex with.

_____ I feel obligated to do well during sex, and I get upset when I have trouble with erection.

_____ My job is creating many pressures that are getting me down and making me feel powerless.

_____ I worry that I am getting old and losing my sexual potency.

_____ I've recently started having erection problems, but I don't have any idea why.

Suggested Action: These are among the most typical causes of erectile troubles. Read through all of this chapter carefully and see what you can learn from it. Then choose the exercises from the remainder of the chapter that seem to suit you best. The important thing is for you to learn how to relax with sex again.

_____ The relationship between my partner and me has been going downhill, and erection problems have been occurring.

_____ When I do go limp, I feel really embarrassed and have trouble talking about it with my partner.

_____ If my partner and I get "discovered," we could be in big trouble.

_____ I often feel guilty about having sex with this person. I'm not sure it is right for us.

_____ My partner has hurt me recently, and I'm still hurting.

_____ My partner doesn't seem to know quite what kind of sexual stimulation feels good to me, and I've been hesitant to ask for anything specific.

——— My partner and I seem to have drifted apart sexually, and both of us have lost interest.

Suggested Action: The quality of a relationship and of the communication in that relationship are key factors in having a happy, successful sex life together. The first few chapters of this book may help you understand this. If you and your partner need to work on communication, Chapter 2 may be of help. If your partnership problems are long-standing or complicated, seeking help from a counselor or therapist would be wise (see Chapter 7). The exercises that follow may help you resolve whatever problems with erection you may be having that stem from conflicts in your relationship.

Your plan of action

After completing these two questionnaires, it is time to make some decisions about how you want to work on your erection difficulties. Nobody can force you to deal with the problem; you're going to have to *want* to do it. Try planning some steps. Here is a checklist of ideas to take into consideration. Pick the ones that seem to fit your situation and give yourself a rough timetable to follow.

Check the things you need to do, or might want to do.	Establish your timetable.
——— See a physician to check out possible physical causes. Make an appointment.	Appointment date and time: ———
——— Read Chapters 2 and 3 in this book regarding communication and getting to know my own body.	To be completed by: ———
——— Explain to a partner what I am attempting to accomplish and find out whether the partner is willing to be involved.	Will do this on: ———————

____ Work with the self-help approaches described on pages 122–132 of this chapter.	Will work on this from ____ to ____ (Allow yourself a minimum of 2 weeks; much more if necessary.)
____ Involve my partner in working with the exercises on pages 132–139 of this chapter.	Will work on this from ____ to ____ (Give yourselves plenty of time.)
____ Find a counselor or sex therapist to consult if things don't go as I hope (Chapter 7).	Who: ____ When: ____
____ No use putting things off any longer, I'm ready to get to work.	When: *Now*

PHASE ONE: DEVELOPING ERECTILE CONFIDENCE ON YOUR OWN

This section will give you some approaches to help you deal with erection problems on your own. Eventually you will probably need to do some exercises with a partner, and the final section of the chapter offers suggestions for accomplishing that. Before you begin improving things with a partner, though, there are plenty of things you can do by yourself.

These self-help exercises are designed to get you started in four important new directions:

1. Avoiding the trap of thinking you are a powerless failure.
2. Learning how to relax and enjoy your sexual arousal.
3. Giving yourself permission to enjoy whatever level of sexual excitement you reach, with or without an erection.
4. Avoiding the kind of pressure and penis watching that can

make you overly concerned about how well you are "performing."

Incidentally, none of the exercises in this chapter can offer you any guarantees that you will always get an erection when you want one. No man can be absolutely certain that his penis will snap to attention on demand. However, these exercises may help you to relax with yourself and your partner and gain enough confidence, so that you will be able to have an erection most of the time, provided that conditions are right for you. And they should also help you feel more comfortable during those times when your penis doesn't respond quite the way you hope.

If you know that your erection problems have grown out of some other sex-related difficulty—such as discouragement over always ejaculating too soon (see Chapter 4) or an inability to reach orgasm (see Chapter 6) or communication trouble in your relationship (see Chapter 2)—then you may have to work on that difficulty first, or along with, the erection concern. Start with whatever aspect of your sexuality makes the most sense.

■ Talking yourself up instead of down

When males experience difficulty getting an erection a few times, they often begin talking to themselves in very negative ways. Their heads play a real number on them. You would be surprised at how important the ways we talk to ourselves may be in determining how our bodies react to different situations. We are what we think we are, and we react to our surroundings accordingly.

Pat had to give up on sex several times because his penis wouldn't get hard. He said all the wrong things to himself and managed to set himself up for several months of erection problems. Without quite putting his thoughts into nice clear sentences, he was making the following assumptions about himself and his sex life:

> Now something is wrong with me, and I'm going to go limp every time.

Not getting a full erection is bad, and it means that my attempt at sex has failed.

This whole thing is too embarrassing and too personal to talk about.

If you have encountered erectile trouble, it is likely that you also made one or all of the same assumptions. Think about it for a few minutes. How do you talk to yourself about erections and not getting them? Be cautious not to trap yourself into making assumptions that are based only on more faulty thinking.

As you think about it now, and whenever your penis doesn't get as erect as you would like, try to talk to yourself about it with some new points of view. Interrupt your negative, failure-oriented thinking with statements like:

I can't expect my penis to get hard as a rock every time I do something sexual.

I can have fun with sex and please a partner, regardless of whether or not I have an erection.

My penis didn't get hard *this* time, but it will another time, provided I'm relaxed and in the mood for sex.

Lack of erection is something that almost all men have experienced. It's nothing to be ashamed of.

I can talk about it and get out my feelings, instead of letting them get dammed up inside.

These statements are all based on facts rather than sexual myths and assumptions. Don't let yourself be fooled by the false ideas on erection that are so often a part of the manhood myth. The more you are able to escape these silly assumptions, the more your body and penis will be freed to function normally in response to sexual arousal.

■ Relax and enjoy yourself: 3-2-1

For many people, it doesn't make much sense to talk about relaxing during sex. After all, sexual arousal causes the muscles of our bodies to become taut with tension. However, if that tension becomes connected to negative emotions, or turns into a desperate, pressured struggle to succeed, it hinders sexual arousal and the enjoyment of sex. There is a simple relaxation exercise that you can practice and build into yourself so that it will be there when you need it. In Chapter 3 an overall body relaxation method was used prior to body touching, and you may wish to review that method before trying this one:

Step 1—selective relaxation of muscle groups. Sit in a comfortable chair, with your back straight. Place your body in as relaxed a position as possible, so that when completely relaxed you will not have to support parts of the body. You are alternately going to contract and relax several different muscle groups in your body. It may be difficult at first, since we are often not used to having just one area of the body tense while the rest is relaxed. With practice it will become easier.

Begin with your feet. Tense them while trying to keep your legs and the other muscles of your body relaxed. Hold your foot muscles contracted for three or four seconds, then relax them as completely as possible. Do not move on until you feel all of the tension gone from your feet, which should take only a few seconds. Now repeat this procedure with each of the following muscle groups, being as careful as possible to contract only that group and not other body parts. Relax each group completely before moving to the next:

> lower legs (calves), one at a time
> upper legs (thighs), one at a time
> buttocks
> lower abdomen
> upper chest
> hands (make a fist)
> upper arms (biceps and triceps), one at a time
> shoulders (shrug them)
> neck (tilt your head backwards)
> jaw (grimace with your mouth)
> upper facial and scalp muscles

Step 2—using a 3-2-1 counting technique. After completing this systematic tensing and relaxing of muscles, tense *all* of your muscles together. Then, as you say the numbers 3-2-1 slowly out loud, relax each of three major portions of your body. The number 3 is the relaxation signal for your head and neck region; 2 is for your trunk, arms, and hands; 1 is for your legs and feet. After you have said the three numbers, your body should feel fully relaxed. If you can detect leftover tension anywhere, work to get rid of it.

Step 3—practice. Over a period of several days, take a few minutes each day to practice this method. Eventually you should try thinking the numbers to yourself rather than saying them aloud. You may want to practice using the technique in situations where you begin to feel a little tense; no one will notice what you're doing. Whenever you feel inner signals of tension (they often show up in your head, stomach, hands, or chest), use the simple 3-2-1 counting method to help your body relax. Keep your breathing regular and somewhat shallow. This will probably prevent your mind from beginning to race with anxious thoughts as well.

From time to time in later exercises, I will suggest that you use this 3-2-1 technique to get calmed down. It should relax your body without detracting from sexual arousal. It should also free you to enjoy your sexual feelings. For now, anytime you are thinking about sex and begin to worry about not getting an erection (or any other problem), try the 3-2-1 and get yourself relaxed right then. This is good training for learning how to stay relaxed and in control during typically tense situations.

■ Indulge yourself

In this exercise you should give yourself permission to be thoroughly selfish in enjoying your body's pleasant sensations. You will probably get an erection during the activities, but if you don't, it is nothing to worry about. You should have a room available that will be private and free from interruptions. It should be warm enough so that you can be comfortable in the nude, and have a bed or carpet with pillows so that you can recline. You may want to have some music playing in the background. During the days when you are doing this exercise, you should avoid masturbating or other sexual activity leading to orgasm. The exercise has six steps:

1. (Optional) If there is some activity that may be counted on to put you in a sexy mood, you may want to give it a try before going on with the exercise. For example, maybe you would like to take in a sexy movie or stroll in the park—whatever works for you.

2. Put yourself in a positive frame of mind about doing the exercise. Read ahead right now so that you know what you're going to be doing. Anticipate it; plan it; look forward to it. Keep in mind that it will be an enjoyable time of experiencing your body and sexual feelings. If you feel any anxiety or tension about the activities, use your 3-2-1 relaxation technique.

3. Immediately prior to the next step, take a relaxing hot bath or shower. If you are sitting in a bath, lie back and let your penis float and move around in the water. Notice what it feels like. Swirl the water around your sex organs or squeeze a washcloth above them so that the water dribbles over your penis and scrotum, again noting the sensations. If you are showering, allow the water to play on your sex organs and feel it dribble off the end of your penis. Whirlpool baths or hand-held shower attachments may add versatility to these bathing activities. Dry thoroughly when finished.

4. After bathing and drying, go directly to your private room and recline on the bed or carpeting, completely nude. Have available several things to enhance your sexy feelings. If pornographic or "nudie" pictures turn you on, have them available. Sexy books may also help. If you get off on rubber or leather goods, women's underwear (or men's), or any other objects or materials, have them with you. If you have a feather, blow dryer for hair, and vibrator handy, get them too. You may also want some massage oil.

5. Your only task is to stimulate your body and sex organs in new and interesting ways. *You are not trying to get an erection or ejaculation.* While doing so, you may look at your sexy pictures, read the sexy book, or whatever you wish. Use the feather to trace lightly over your skin, including the sex organs. Where does it feel most sensitive? Turn the blow dryer on cool or warm and play the stream of air over different body parts. Concentrate on the sex organs and see how the air feels on them. Use the vibrator lightly on your body if you wish. Try new forms of touching with your fingers and hands, using massage oils or even talcum powder. Relax, lie back, and enjoy any pleasurable sensations you generate.

6. Do *not* go any further for the time being. Even if you get turned on, avoid stimulating yourself to orgasm. Just enjoy the feeling of being aroused, and—if you have one—enjoy your erection. Eventually, when you feel finished, get dressed and go on about your daily life. You may want to repeat this entire exercise several times if you enjoy it. In any case, you should try it *at least* twice, on two different days. When you feel ready, move on to the next exercise.

■ Easy come—easy go

What goes up must come down, and every erection will eventually come down. That is how penises work. In any single sexual encounter, a man's penis may gain and lose degrees of erection several times. The important thing to remember is that losing your erection from time to time is natural and expectable; it doesn't mean that you won't be able to get the erection back. This exercise is designed to help you become more comfortable and relaxed with *losing* an erection. It is suggested that you do not masturbate or have other sexual activity to orgasm during the days when you plan to do this exercise.

1. *Getting an erection.* In as relaxed a manner as possible, stimulate your penis and body in ways that will tend to help you get an erection. If you got an erection easily in the preceding exercise ("Indulge yourself," page 126), then repeat those activities. You should not have to struggle too hard to make

your penis hard—no desperate rubbing or pulling. The more calm, gentle, and consistent you can be in your stimulating movements, the better. You don't have to achieve a full, rock-hard erection. If you need some extra help, using some type of vibrator on your penis will probably lend some new and useful sensations.

2. *Losing the erection.* When you have achieved the maximum erection you seem to be going to have (*don't ejaculate*), stop stimulating yourself and let your penis go as limp as possible. If it refuses to go soft, walking around will probably help it along. You can also give the head of your penis a good, firm squeeze to help things along.

3. *Assessing your situation.* Now look at your soft penis and feel it with your hands. Say to yourself something like this: "It got hard, and I let it get soft. So what—it's soft. But I know it got hard before, and it will get hard again. There is nothing wrong with my penis just because it goes limp for a while. It's supposed to do that anyway."

4. *Repeat the procedure.* Go ahead and restimulate yourself to some degree of erection again and allow yourself the male privilege of getting soft again. That is what this exercise is all about: giving yourself *permission* to lose an erection. It is no reflection on your character or manliness. The entire exercise should be repeated until you feel comfortable and confident with it, a minimum of two times on different days.

■ **Avoiding penis watching**

The trouble with many men who have continuing trouble with erections is that they are constantly "on stage" for themselves during sex. They are always "watching" their penises and are constantly wondering, "How am I doing? Is it getting hard? Am I pleasing my partner?" There are some common sense ways of getting our heads preoccupied with things other than our sexual "performance."

If you masturbate, try to find some method of distracting

yourself from constant penis watching. Some suggestions follow, but use your own imagination to invent other possibilities. To whatever degree possible, they should be ideas that you could also use during sexual activity with a partner.

While masturbating (not necessarily to orgasm), really listen to some music, listen to your breathing, look at some pictures that are pleasing to you, allow yourself to fantasize about some sexy scenes (real or totally imaginary), or simply allow yourself to feel your skin sensations fully. These distractions should not pull you away too far from enjoying your sexual arousal. They are there to prevent you from being preoccupied with penis watching. Try to learn to let your penis take care of itself. With appropriate stimulation, it can get along very nicely without your looking down at it.

■ The power of fantasy

When you relax, close your eyes, and give your imagination permission to find its own direction, you'll find you may generate some surprising fantasies. Psychologists and counselors know that you often face things about yourself in fantasy that you are unable to face in reality. Fantasy is also effective in training yourself to meet particular situations that may later occur in real life. Both of the suggestions for directed fantasy that follow can help you gain erectile confidence. Sit back, get your body relaxed, and close your eyes. Read through the suggestions for each fantasy thoroughly before beginning. Then set your imagination to work visualizing the scene as vividly as possible in your "mind's eye."

1. *Your inner power.* In this first fantasy, visualize yourself naked, as accurately as possible. Don't lie to yourself about your body's appearance. It might even be a good idea, if you want, to exaggerate some of your body's features that you particularly dislike. If you think your nose is too big, fantasize that you have a nose twice as long as it really is. If you don't like the extra fat around your middle, imagine yourself with a huge beer belly, hanging down in front. If you think your

penis is too small, imagine it to be the size of a pea. If you think your legs are too skinny, visualize them as toothpicks.

Then imagine that deep inside your body is an undiscovered reserve of power and strength. Find where it is located in *your* body and see it in your fantasy with as much detail as you can. After you have located this power reserve and know what it looks like to your imagination, imagine the power being released and flowing outward into all parts of your body. Watch it move into your head, chest, arms, sex organs, and legs. In your fantasy imagine that your body comes alive with its new-found strength and power. You feel good: energetic, enthused, happy. Your body swells with energy and glows. See it in your mind as clearly as you can and enjoy it.

2. *Losing your erection.* In this second fantasy, you should imagine being with a partner and wanting to share sexual activity with that person. Set it up carefully in your mind. All of the conditions are right. You are both turned on and ready to go. Then visualize that just as you are about to really get it on, your penis goes limp. Stay in touch with how your body feels during the fantasy. If you feel any anxiety, fear, or tension nagging at you, use the 3-2-1 relaxation technique described on page 124. It is important to remain relaxed.

Carefully visualize all of the positive things you can do in such a situation:

> You're not embarrassed.
>
> You don't apologize or make excuses.
>
> The two of you enjoy playing with your soft penis.
>
> You offer to provide your partner with other forms of sexual stimulation.

Eventually, fantasize that your erection returns. What you do with it then is up to your own imagination.

You may find through using these self-help approaches that you develop enough confidence in your erections and regaining them that you will feel ready to go ahead and try things out with a partner. That is fine, as long as you have the kind of communication patterns with the other person that will enable you to discuss your feelings and your sexual relationship freely. Some of the early exercises in the following section can help establish this type of communication.

In any case, *take your time*. Don't rush yourself in any of these exercises. The whole point is to develop confidence, and that doesn't happen in one easy lesson. When you feel ready to begin involving a partner in the process of gaining erectile confidence, move on to the next section.

PHASE TWO: GAINING ERECTILE CONFIDENCE WITH A PARTNER

The preceding chapter offered basic approaches to be kept in mind when working on sex problems with a partner. It would be a good idea to look them over now, on pages 99–100. Also look again at the suggestions found in Chapter 2 for improving communication. What you are trying to do is figure out the best way to get your partner to help you.

■ Establishing the ground rules

It may be that your partner knows you are working on improving your erection and is willing to cooperate in the exercise. If so, skip this initial activity and go on to the next set of exercises.

This first exercise is designed to help you think through the way to approach another person to help you, and the way to establish the necessary ground rules for working together. If you have a spouse or sexual partner of long duration, you may already have a good base of mutual understanding and communication from which to work. I have also had male clients who lacked regular sexual partners and therefore sought out partners who were willing to work with them on resolving erectile problems. This sometimes developed into a lasting relationship; other times the two parted company once the difficulty was resolved. It will be up to you to secure an appropriate sexual partner with whom you feel relaxed and comfortable.

1. The first step is to explain what has been going on and what you are going to need. Here are some of the basics that you may want to include:

> You have been having some difficulty getting a full erection during sex. (*Remember*: no apologies necessary.)

> With this sort of thing, it's easy to get into a vicious circle of getting tense about the problem, so then it happens again.

> You are learning how to relax more with sex so that erections will happen naturally, *and so that when you don't get an erection it won't be such a big deal.*

> You have been going through a step-by-step procedure to become accustomed to relaxed sex and now need to start trying things out with a partner.

> You are not going to make any guarantees about how things will go, nor are you going to place a lot of expectations or "performance" standards on yourself.

> Talking things over at each stage and being able to share feelings is going to be an important part of the process.

2. After you have discussed some of these ideas, and perhaps others, let your partner read this book, particularly the parts with which you have been working. The other individual should understand the principles discussed early in this chapter and know what self-help exercises you have been using up till now. Honesty and openness are essential if the two of you are to work successfully on this together. The partner should also read the remainder of this chapter so that she or he will understand what exercises the two of you will be doing. Although doubts and fears are to be expected for both of you, don't proceed together until your partner feels ready and willing and until the two of you have discussed your plan of action.

■ Relaxing together

In a private location that will be free from interruption, the two of you should do the relaxation exercise described on pages 124–126. If you have already mastered the technique, teach it to your partner. Be certain to include the selective contracting and relaxing of major muscle groups and the 3-2-1 overall body relaxation method. The exercise should be done with both of you fully clothed.

■ Enjoying each other's bodies

This is the same mutual body-pleasuring exercise that I suggested in the last chapter, but I am repeating it here to avoid confusion. Again, the whole point is to relax together without having to worry about how your penis is responding.

Both of you should remove all of your clothing and, if you both enjoy it, undress each other slowly. If you're not used to doing this, it may seem a little silly or embarrassing, so if you feel like laughing, just be careful not to laugh *at*, only *with*.

You might also want to bathe or shower together, soaping each other's backs, washing each other's hair, and so on. Dry each other off when you finish. Relax together and have a good time. The one rule for this entire exercise is that *neither* of you should touch the other's sex organs. You are not going to end up doing anything sexual. I just want you to relax and enjoy your bodies together.

In a warm, comfortable, private place, dim the lights if you wish and put on some relaxing music. Then take turns touching and massaging each other. Remember: *avoid the sex organs*, and make a special effort to be gentle and caring as you trace, stroke, and massage fingers and hands over the other's body. The one being touched need only relax and *fully enjoy* all of the pleasant sensations. If you find a particular way of being touched unpleasant, suggest that your partner try something a little different. Avoid such strong negative messages as "Don't do that," or "I don't like it that way." Instead, say something positive, like "How about a little lighter touch there, and maybe a circular motion." As you're being touched, don't let your mind be charged with thoughts about how you are going to "pay" the other person back or other worries. Be selfish and enjoy all the attention you're getting. When it is your turn to touch your partner, simply do what feels good and right to you and take whatever suggestions your partner offers.

Both of you may get sexually aroused by all of this touching, and that is fine. But it is also okay not to get turned on. Sexual arousal is not the goal of this exercise. If you do get aroused, be sure *not* to have sex together right then. That shouldn't happen until after you've worked on other exercises later. The next exercises are aimed at developing further confidence in your erectile capabilities.

You may do the mutual touching for as long as you both find it pleasurable. I suggest a minimum of twenty minutes for the entire exercise—ten minutes for each of you to be touched. I also suggest that you do the exercise a *minimum of two times* over a period of at least two days, before progressing to the next stage. You may want to spend several days with the mutual body pleasuring, depending on how long it takes for both of you to feel really relaxed and comfortable with each other. Remember to talk over any tensions, embarrassments, and other feelings that come up, including the good ones.

■ Nongenital guiding

After you have had a chance to feel comfortable with the preceding exercise, you should add a new dimension, *guiding*. As the two of you are stroking and massaging each other's bodies (still avoiding the sex organs), the person who is being stimulated gently guides his or her partner's hands. Silently, your hands on your partner's, demonstrate the sorts of nongenital touching that feel best to your body. Help your partner to know how heavily or lightly to stroke you, what parts to concentrate on and what to avoid, and what motions are the most pleasurable. As you are guiding your partner's hands, help them to relax and be free of tension or self-consciousness. Take time to enjoy the special pleasure that guiding can give to your own body and to your partner's. Afterwards, talk over your thoughts and feelings.

You should use this guiding technique at least twice, on more than one day. Do not have any further sexual activity during this period.

■ A game

This exercise should be done before progressing to specific genital stimulation. It may be done on its own or immediately after either of the nongenital body-pleasuring exercises that have already been described.

For the exercise, your penis should not have an erection. Your partner should gently handle your nonerect penis, feeling it, looking at it, exploring it. The game is for you *not* to get an erection, as you both learn to feel comfortable with your limp penis. If you get an erection, walk around or otherwise distract yourself so that it will go away. If it just won't go away long enough for you to do the exercise, that really isn't a problem, but you may as well give up on this one for now.

■ Genital guiding, erection, and losing it

The surroundings and relaxed atmosphere for this exercise should be the same as that used in the other body-pleasuring activities. You may wish to take turns, but I am only going to describe the stimulation that is to be given to males. Both you and your partner should be naked and in comfortable positions. You should be reclining, and your partner may sit facing you with legs over yours, or simply be seated beside you.

1. This time, your hands will guide your partner's in stimulating your sex organs. Begin by guiding your partner's hands in a gentle exploration and caressing of your scrotum and penis. Using some K-Y jelly or massage oil may well enhance the sensations. Teach your partner how to stroke your penis in a sexually arousing manner. Pay attention to how tightly your penis is gripped, how rapidly it is stroked, and how far up and down the hand should go during stroking. Be selfish; let your partner know what feels best to you.

2. Getting an erection is the next step in this exercise. It may be that the guided stimulation has already produced a hardening of your penis. If it is sufficiently hard, you may go directly to the third step. You may, however, want to incorporate some of the sexually arousing stimuli that you used by yourself earlier. Use pictures, objects, vibrators, or any aid your partner is comfortable with. Oral stimulation may work especially well if your partner is willing to provide it. You may want to tell your partner the kinds of mouth stimulation that seem most effective to you. Enjoy whatever erection you get, but do not ejaculate. If you do not get an erection, back up a few steps and repeat the nongenital body-pleasuring exercises. Then, come back to this exercise another day.

3. Finally, allow yourself to lose your erection. Simply stop stimulating the penis and let the erection go away, or have your partner give the head of your penis a firm squeeze. When the penis is soft, resume the sexually stimulating touching and see if you can get the erection back again. You may want to repeat this once or twice so that both of you become relaxed and comfortable with your losing and regaining an erection. Do not have an orgasm this time, and talk over your feelings.

■ For your partner

Your partner may feel somewhat left out of this whole process, so you may want to decide on some forms of stimulation that will be pleasurable for her or him, possibly including an orgasm.

Your partner should teach you what kinds of manual and/or oral stimulation are especially pleasurable for her or him. Find out what sexual activities your partner enjoys that do *not* require that you have an erect penis. The two of you should be developing strategies so that anytime your penis loses its erection, sex does not have to cease. You can share enjoyable, intimate, and orgasmic sexual encounters whether or not you have an erection. In fact, you may choose to share some of these other forms of sex even when your penis *will* stay hard.

■ Erection and intercourse

If you have been using these exercises to improve your erections for sexual intercourse with a woman, this exercise should be your next step. Be sure that you both feel that the earlier exercises have been relaxed and successful before moving to this stage. The point of this exercise is to help you become more comfortable with your erect penis inside your partner's vagina and not to panic if you temporarily lose your erection during intercourse. Avoid masturbating during the period of time when you are working on intercourse.

Lie down and ask your female partner to face you and straddle your thighs, just behind your penis. She then stimulates you with her hands, mouth, or other aid that has proved successful during previous exercises in producing an erection. Both of you should take your time. Now is the time to use your 3-2-1 relaxation method if you begin to feel tense or anxious. Also, use the self-help techniques you learned to avoid "penis watching"—listen to music, become aware of your partner's breathing, or focus on the pleasant sensations you are experiencing.

When your partner believes that you have a good firm erection, she crouches over your penis and guides it into her vagina, gradually settling down on it. A lubricant may be important here so that there is no fumbling or uncomfortable sticking as your penis glides into her vagina. She then moves her body up and down, stimulating your penis. You should keep your own thrusting at a minimum for now. You may signal her to move off from your penis anytime you want. If you lose your erection, simply return to the other forms of stimulation that have been successful. You should plan *not* to ejaculate the first two or three times you do this exercise. The point is to spend some time in the vagina with an erection, nothing more. You should do this exercise two or three times over a one-week period, or longer if you prefer. Eventually, when you both feel ready and your erection is lasting, you may choose to have an orgasm.

After things are going well with this female-on-top position for intercourse, and you feel confident with your erection, you may want to experiment with other positions. A natural progression is to start intercourse with the female on top, then both moving to your sides. Eventually, you will feel ready for the male-on-top position, if you want to use it. Take your time and feel comfortable with each new position before moving on.

Other forms of sharing

If you have been trying to gain erectile confidence for use in sexual activities with another man, or any shared activity other than vaginal intercourse, the principles for continuing are the same. Move along gradually. Whenever you lose your erection, back up a little to a form of stimulation that you know works.

If you go limp—some reminders

Keep in mind that most men occasionally lose their erections during sex. That is nothing to be surprised or ashamed about. It is no reflection on your masculinity or sexual prowess. If your partner believes that sex can be good only when you have a rock-hard erection, that is her or his problem. You don't need to apologize. If you feel you need to say anything, try something to the point, such as "Well, I guess this isn't my night. How about trying this. . . ." Then you can back up to some other form of mutual stimulation that you both can enjoy. However, if you do feel a little scared or embarrassed, go ahead and tell your partner. Those feelings are nothing to be ashamed of either. Try to encourage the sort of communication in which you can talk to each other about all of your feelings. If you can relax and accept occasional erection problems as a part of life, you won't get trapped into a vicious circle of tension that will continue to spoil sex for you.

Finally, one of the foremost rules to keep in mind is that you should not have sex unless it is something you *want* to do. Don't be pushed into sex by the demands of others or by your own need to prove something. Attempting sex when you're not in the mood is a good way of asking for trouble.

6

─━◆━─

Other Sex Problems

This chapter takes a look at several ways in which a man may lose sexual enjoyment unless he takes some action.

WHEN YOU WANT TO COME—
BUT CAN'T

Rick had been a member of a men's discussion group that had met for several weeks. I visited the group as an outside consultant on male sexuality. During the discussion following my talk, Rick spoke to the group about a sex problem. "I don't understand what happens to me sometimes," he complained. "I'll be having sex and feel ready to ejaculate, but I just can't get over the top. I'll be turned on, and have no problems staying hard, but won't reach orgasm. Once in a while when this happens, if I work hard, I'll eventually come, but usually I have to give up. I can always masturbate myself to orgasm after, though. Some of the women I have sex with think it's great that I can just keep on pumping, but it gets damn frustrating for me not to be able to come when I want to. Sometimes my partners seem disappointed, too. One woman even told me she felt a little cheated. I don't know what to do about this, and I'm afraid the problem is getting worse."

Professional sex therapists used to think that it was rare for a man to have difficulty reaching orgasm if he had no trouble keeping an erection. However, as more and more males bring their sex-related worries to therapists, *delayed ejaculation* or *ejaculatory incompetence* (as the condition is called) is being recognized as more common than was previously suspected. Many men may experience ejaculatory trouble once or twice in a lifetime, some may have difficulty more often, but only a few may never be able to reach orgasm in any manner, including masturbation. This problem should not be confused with the situation in which a man actually experiences the sensations of orgasm but has no ejaculation. This more medical problem is discussed later in this chapter under *dry ejaculation* (page 165).

The most common form of delayed ejaculation, as I shall call it, occurs when a man has difficulty ejaculating while having intercourse with a woman. Yet once he withdraws his penis from the woman's vagina, he has no problem reaching orgasm through some other form of sexual stimulation. Delayed ejaculation does show up in other ways as well. Here are some examples, drawn from the stories of men who have discussed their concerns with me:

> A forty-four-year-old married man who could not reach orgasm in about half of his sexual encounters with his wife.

> A gay college student who had difficulty ejaculating during any sexual activity while lying on his back, but was never troubled when taking a more active, on-top role.

> A twenty-seven-year-old who could not reach orgasm in any way as long as a woman was in the room with him. During intercourse, he would sometimes fake the

bodily movements of orgasm to protect himself from embarrassment.

A twenty-one-year-old college senior who had never been able to produce an ejaculation at all, except in wet dreams when he was asleep.

Each of these men found that the exercises, described later in this chapter, enabled him to begin having orgasms whenever he wished. The exercises can work for you, too, but be sure to read the next few sections before trying them.

What gets in the way?

There are many psychological blocks that may keep you from "letting go" fully and reaching orgasm. For example, Brian was brought up with strong religious values telling him that sex was wrong. At the age of eighteen, his girl friend had become pregnant in one of their first sexual encounters. It was not surprising, then, when his sex-related guilt and fears of pregnancy began to interfere with his sex life at the age of twenty-one. He found it impossible to reach orgasm during intercourse, although he never had any trouble getting and keeping his erection.

Joel was a tense and controlled person in every respect of his life. He could laugh but never lose himself to laughter. He never cried, never lost his temper. The more we talked about his difficulty with delayed ejaculation, the more it became obvious that to him an orgasm represented a surrendering to his emotions, which he considered an almost disgusting thing to think about doing. It scared him too, because he didn't like to feel "out of control" in the presence of another person. So even though he longed for sexual intimacy and frequently had sex with partners, he was never able just to let himself go in the end in order to have an orgasm. Sometimes he couldn't even ejaculate when he masturbated.

The cases of Brian and Joel are typical of those who have trouble reaching orgasm. Often the problem occurs because of a conflict between the two partners. Anger, hostility, and resentment may all play a part in holding back a man's orgasm. A man may wish to frustrate or anger his partner, another example of letting his penis do all of his talking. Masters and Johnson have reported cases in which a man began to have delayed ejaculation following some upsetting event, such as being punished for masturbating or finding his partner in bed with another man. At what point such negative circumstances will affect a man's sexual responsiveness is unpredictable. Some men are not affected at all. Others may have erection problems. But for some the target of the stress is orgasm, and the man finds it difficult or impossible to reach the point of ejaculation.

If delayed ejaculation is troubling you to any degree, there are ways for you to work on the problem—alone and with your partner. The principles that are behind the exercises are simple. Most men have some degree of orgasmic ability, and the exercises build on that. The man who cannot reach orgasm at all must first learn how to produce one, then build on that ability.

Where to begin

Read through each of the following descriptions and decide which one sounds the most like your own situation. With each description are some suggestions for how to work on the problem.

Description 1: No matter what kind of sexual stimulation I try, I never reach orgasm.

> If you do not even have orgasms and ejaculations in your sleep ("wet dreams"), or if you have been experiencing other kinds of sexual or body problems, you should first get a thorough medical examination from a qualified physician, preferably one who knows something about sexual problems. When ejaculation *never* occurs, no matter what you do, it is best to seek the help of a professional sex therapist (see page 195). If this is impossible, careful reading of this entire book and working on the exercises in this chapter may be

of some help. Your first step will be to find some way to have an orgasm, and that will mean relaxing and giving yourself permission to do so. But outside professional help will probably be your best bet.

Description 2: The only way I can reach orgasm is through masturbation, seldom (or never) in the presence of my partner.

Begin working with the Level 1 exercises on page 144.

Description 3: I can reach orgasm with my partner present, but only (or usually) through self-stimulation and not by my partner's efforts to stimulate me.

Begin working with the Level 2 exercises on page 146.

Description 4: I can usually reach orgasm through masturbation or my partner's hand stimulation, but I cannot reach orgasm in some activity we both want to share (such as intercourse or oral sex).

Begin working with the Level 3 exercises on page 147.

Description 5: Just occasionally, I don't reach orgasm during some sexual activity with my partner. It's not a big problem, but a little annoying and frustrating.

Begin working with the Level 4 exercises on page 149.

■ **Learning how to relax and avoid penis watching**

As you work on exercises to help with delayed ejaculation, it is a good idea to know how to relax in a hurry and how to distract yourself so you aren't constantly wondering how you're doing. In the last chapter, several steps were given for learning a *3-2-1 Relaxation Technique* and some hints were mentioned for getting your mind off your own performance. Turn back to pages 124 and 129 to review these ideas if you have not already learned them well.

LEVEL 1
(*Goal:* To reach orgasm with a partner present.)

Some males have trouble reaching orgasm with a partner present, regardless of type of stimulation. If you are stuck here, your first step will be to ejaculate with your partner watching. Reaching that step can occur in three stages:

1. *Fantasy.* In a relaxing and private location, at a time when your partner isn't around, lie back and start masturbating. Take your time. Enjoy all of the pleasant sensations of sexual arousal. During the masturbation, close your eyes and see yourself masturbating in your imagination. As you continue to masturbate, imagine that your partner enters the room. Notice how this fantasy makes you feel. Take your time as you imagine your partner coming closer and closer to you, watching you masturbate. The goal of this exercise is to reach actual orgasm while fantasizing that your partner is watching you. If you find yourself having trouble ejaculating, then imagine your partner turning around and not watching or temporarily leaving the room until you feel yourself about to reach orgasm. Then you can imagine the partner reappearing just at the moment you ejaculate, or just after. Use this fantasy while masturbating as often as you must to be able to get to the point of feeling comfortable with the idea of your partner watching you at the time of your ejaculation. There should be no rush to move on. Take several days with these exercises. If you have orgasms too frequently during this training process, they may just get that much more difficult to have.

2. *Involving your partner.* The idea is to reach orgasm as your partner watches. Communication and accurate information are the keys to this partner cooperation. Try to establish an easy two-way communication (see Chapter 2). Be certain that your partner reads this chapter thoroughly and understands what you are attempting to accomplish. Your partner has the right *not* to cooperate in the process. Talk together and find out what you both really want from each other. If you don't seem to be getting anywhere, or if conflicts keep cropping up between you, it's probably time to seek help from a counselor.

3. *Living out your fantasy.* After getting together with your partner about what you are trying to accomplish, it is time to

begin. Start by relaxing and getting in a sexy mood. Then begin masturbating. To help you, your partner should plan to look away, or even leave the room, while you continue masturbating. Arrange a signal, so that when you are just about to ejaculate, you can tell your partner to turn around (or return to the room) in time to watch your orgasm with you. If you still run into the problem of not being able to ejaculate, have your partner go away and try again.

Once you have been able to ejaculate in your partner's presence, you have gone a long way toward improving your problem with delayed ejaculation. Over a period of days, keep experimenting with this exercise and have your partner spend more and more time with you while you masturbate. Don't push yourself to do this more often than you would typically have sex, or you may experience trouble ejaculating simply because you're not very turned on. Also, your partner may get aroused by watching you, so the two of you may want to work out ways of giving your partner sexual satisfaction that do not (yet) require an orgasm from you.

When you feel comfortable reaching orgasm while your partner watches, you are ready to move on to the exercises in Level 2.

LEVEL 2
(*Goal:* To reach orgasm through a partner's stimulation.)

The next important step for those who experience delayed ejaculation is to be relaxed about having your partner bring you to orgasm.

If you can already masturbate to orgasm with your partner present, the best way to proceed is as follows. While you masturbate, your partner should put a hand on top of yours and leave it there while you produce your own orgasm. If all goes well, try the same thing again another day, but as you feel you are about to ejaculate, let go of your penis and have your partner provide the final stroke(s) to make you ejaculate. If this doesn't work, back up, start stimulating yourself again to the point of orgasm, and try to have your partner take over again just in time to make you come.

Some men find other forms of stimulation by partners helpful too. Ask your partner to try as long as it gives you no problems in ejaculating. The point is to have an orgasm that is produced by your partner. Once you have achieved success with this goal, repeat it over a period of several days, until longer periods of stimulation by your partner produce your orgasm every time. When you are ready, move on to the next level.

LEVEL 3
(*Goal:* To reach orgasm during a desirable shared sexual activity with your partner.)

This is your final goal. Most men with delayed ejaculation want to be able to reach orgasm during intercourse or some other shared activity. If you have worked your way through Levels 1 and 2, or if you are just starting at Level 3, you should be able to have an orgasm most of the time through some type of stimulation by your partner. You know what works for you to this point. Now you can build on that to achieve orgasm with your partner in other ways. Choose the following exercises that seem to fit your own particular situation best:

1. *Enjoying each other's bodies.* It may be important for you and your partner to spend some time relaxing together and enjoying each other's bodies in nonsexual ways. You need to feel comfortable with each other and to develop a real sense of trust together. The suggestions on pages 134–135 in the last chapter can help; give them a try for a few days before going on.

2. *Reaching orgasm during intercourse with a woman.* For this exercise you should be reclining on your back. Your female partner can then sit or crouch between your legs, facing your sex organs, so that she can reach your penis. Both of

you should be nude. The exercise is simple and makes use of everything you have accomplished in earlier exercises (or in your sex life together). Your partner is to stimulate your penis with her hands or mouth, in whatever ways she has been able to bring you to orgasm before. As you get more and more aroused, she should get into position so that she will be able to crouch over you and guide your penis into her vagina with a minimum of effort. It may be wise to use a lubricant on your penis so that entering the vagina can happen quickly. As she continues to stimulate you with hands or mouth, you will reach that point where ejaculation is inevitable. Immediately signal her so that she can guide your penis into her vagina at the moment of your orgasm. The goal, of course, is for you to ejaculate within her vagina, so be certain that the two of you are using effective methods of birth control. If your feeling of being about to ejaculate disappears once you have begun intercourse, your partner should move off from your penis and go back to the kind of stimulation that was working before. Then when you are about to ejaculate again, you can repeat the intercourse maneuver.

Do this exercise over a period of several days. Each time, try having your penis inserted into your partner's vagina at a slightly earlier point, so that you spend progressively more time with intercourse prior to reaching orgasm. If you run into difficulties ejaculating, go back to the exercises on Level 1 or 2 and work from there. As you feel confident with your ability to reach orgasm, you may begin to experiment with other positions for intercourse.

3. *For activities other than intercourse.* If you have been working to achieve orgasm in sexual activities other than vaginal intercourse, the principles remain the same. Have your partner use whatever form of stimulation has brought you to orgasm before. When you reach that feeling of being about to ejaculate, get your penis immediately involved in the other form of sex where you are working to achieve orgasm. Again, the first step toward your final goal is to ejaculate during the

shared activity. Then over a period of days you can gradually increase the amount of time spent in the activity before ejaculating. It can work to help you relax and have orgasms without frustrating delay.

LEVEL 4
(*Goal:* To resolve temporary or occasional problems with delayed ejaculation.)

Although there are no reliable statistics available, many sex therapists have suggested that a high proportion of men probably experience occasional difficulty with delayed ejaculation. The occurrence of the problem may be unpredictable and difficult to understand. If you have only occasional delayed orgasm, here are some suggestions:

1. *Don't panic—communicate.* The more upset you allow yourself to get over this, the more problems it is likely to cause you. Talk with your partner. Be honest about how the delayed ejaculation makes you feel and let your partner tell you the same sorts of things. Sex can often be very good even without an orgasm, so don't invent a problem if there isn't one. Unless your delayed ejaculation is happening often enough to be really frustrating to you or your partner, don't worry about it. However, if it has become a problem, then read over all of the exercises in Levels 1 through 3. These should give you an idea of where you need to begin work on the difficulty.

2. *Be willing to back up.* When you are actually involved in a sexual encounter and are having trouble reaching orgasm, be ready to stop what you are doing and try some other form of stimulation. The exercises in Levels 1, 2, and 3 may hold some suggestions if you need them. Also remember that although having an orgasm feels good, it doesn't "prove" anything about your manhood. If you don't ejaculate, try not to be embarrassed and don't apologize. Face it, talk about it with your partner, and don't panic. Next time, if you keep relaxed about the whole thing, the chances are good that you will have no problems.

GAMESMANSHIP SEX: WHEN SEX IS A
MATTER OF WINNING AND LOSING

Probably one of the saddest things that has happened to sex in our society is the way some people play games, with sex determining who is the winner. We sometimes even use game-oriented terms in reference to sex, such as *scoring*. I was once part of a discussion group in which men talked about their sexual values. One man went into great detail about the many ways in which he could "convince" women to have sex with him. Another fellow remarked that the whole thing sounded like a big game without much feeling behind it. The first man answered him by saying, "Life is a game." Maybe so, but the more that people make sex into a game, the more they set themselves up for trouble.

One-night stands . . . and falls

The singles bar and gay bar are, to a large extent, places in which people meet sexual partners. For some, it is a very casual scene, and the desire is only to share a quick sexual experience with another warm body. For others, the hope is that a partner will be found who will become a true lover for a long period of time. The most common complaint I hear from men who are into one-night stands is that it eventually becomes empty and boring. As one man in his early twenties put it, "I feel as if I'm really missing something. Sometimes I think it would be cheaper and just as much fun to stay home and jerk off. But I yearn for something more, so I go looking for it. Only trouble is, I haven't found it yet."

Life in these bars, or any places where people are looking for casual sex, is usually full of games. Sometimes everybody knows the rules, and sometimes nobody does. Judging from my contacts with people who seek sex therapy, I conclude that the more games that exist between sexual partners, the greater the likelihood of sex-related problems developing.

Persuasion games in sex

For many people, sex becomes a symbol of power or of getting one's own way. It's fun and it feels good, so the game is to persuade someone to "do it." That's winning. For those who want to have sex but don't want to take much responsibility for it, the game may be to be persuaded by someone else so that afterward they can say, "It was all your idea." Sometimes it isn't even sex that they want, but only the satisfaction of "winning the game."

Persuasion games in sex are common. Here are three examples that show up most frequently among males:

EVERYBODY'S DOING IT

Rules of the Game: To persuade your partners that the kind of sex you want to have is going on all around. Everybody is doing it and liking it. If partners aren't interested, they aren't "with it."

To win: Your partner gives you what you want.

YOU OWE IT TO ME

Rules of the Game: To convince partners that for whatever reason you can invent, they owe you a good time with sex. You could suggest that you paid for the wining and dining, so now it's their turn to put out. Or maybe you've been going together for a long enough time that it is "time for sex." Or maybe the partner has been teasing you, so now you can suggest that it is time to get down to business.

To win: Your partner "pays you back" with sex.

THERE'S NO WAY TO STOP NOW

Rules of the Game: To persuade your partners that there is truth to the myth that once a man gets turned on, it's physically harmful for him not to follow through to orgasm. This game is a handy old standby. Talk about pain and blue balls and prostate infections as if you know what you're talking about. If your partner suggests that you go home and masturbate, look shocked and explain that you're not a little boy anymore.

To win: Your partner has sex with you out of sympathy for the physical dangers of your "condition."

These games still work for lots of people. As one man put it: "What's wrong with games? Everybody knows what's going on, so you both play your way toward the bedroom with a minimum of delay." Maybe, but games like these can and do hurt both players. There often is a price to pay in guilt, regret, and hurt. Conquering a sexual partner is a kick in itself for some people, but it can often leave you feeling empty and wondering if you really won at all. You will have to ask yourself what kind of quality you want in your sexual relationships.

What does the sex game prove?

In the competition of everyday life, men sometimes see sex as a way of proving something about themselves or their relationships. Here are some of the common "proof traps" that men fall into with sex:

Trap 1: sex proves I am a man.   For many men, an active penis is a signal of full manhood. They feel most like a "real man" when they have had what they consider to be a good sexual experience. If the opportunity for sex comes along, the manly thing to do is to take advantage of it. I once heard a man say to another that he had decided not to have sex with a woman who had asked him to go to bed with her. He explained that the woman was not his type and that he wanted more than quickie sex. The other man told him that he must have been crazy to turn her down. "A screw is a screw," he argued. The fact is that not all men see sex as the game of whether or not they score, and their feelings of manliness don't depend solely on where their penises have been. Having sex doesn't prove that you're a man.

Trap 2: sex proves we love each other. Sex can be an enjoyable and powerful expression of love but doesn't in itself prove anything about love. When couples fear that love is leaving their relationship or feel insecure with what they have going together, they sometimes turn to sex for reassurance. Paul, a divorced man, said to me, "Sex was the last thing to go in my marriage. We had been drifting farther and farther apart but could always jump into bed and have good sex. I think we used sex to fool ourselves into thinking that we were still okay together, even long after we should have broken up." Some people use the love argument to persuade others to have sex: "If you love me, you'll do it with me." Anytime you have to "prove" your love through sex, I would question the quality of the relationship. Sex can be a great part of a loving relationship, but not the only part.

Trap 3: sex proves I am an adult. Some men never seem to get over the need to prove that they are "grown-up." Teenagers often go through phases where they smoke, drink, have sex, drive fast, or rebel against their parents as ways of showing their increasing adulthood. Then, as they grow up, they are able to put these things into a manageable perspective. Some never quite seem to make it, however, and feel they must go on proving how adult they really are. Sex is one of the things that usually gets involved in the game. Actually age and sex don't have much to do with each other. There are some teenagers who approach their sex lives with a great deal of maturity and intelligence, and there are some middle-aged people who probably aren't ready to handle the responsibilities that go along with sex.

When you want to stop playing the game

If you have been making sex into a game all your life, and you want to stop playing, here are some hints for you:

1. Sex is always a matter of choice. You can decide whether or not to have sex and for many different reasons. Being a self-reliant man means being able to think and choose,

rather than just following your penis or your manhood script.

2. Work to develop self-confidence. A man who feels okay about himself and his life does not have to try "proving" anything through sex. Developing confidence means taking risks and sometimes not succeeding. But risks will also lead to successes and the knowledge of where your strengths and weaknesses lie.

3. Establish good communication with your partner(s). Honesty, openness, and sharing real feelings usually add up to the sort of relationship that doesn't need games. That kind of relationship will stay happy longer than any other kind.

WHEN YOUR INTEREST
IN SEX SAGS

Mitch was in his early forties, and his sex life had all but come to a halt. He rarely felt interested in shared sex, never masturbated, and didn't even think much about it except to wonder why his once-active sex life had faded. "My sex drive seems to be at low ebb," he explained. "I'm afraid that if I go on this way, sex is going to be a thing of the past for me. Yet what is even worse is that I'm not sure I even care very much." There were plenty of reasons behind Mitch's lagging sexual desires. He had recently been divorced, and one of the main problems he and his wife had had was sex. His wife had never cared much for sex, and Mitch had often experienced erection problems or ejaculated too soon. Over the years, sex had become a source of discouragement and bad feelings for him.

Causes of low sexual interests

There are loads of possible reasons behind low levels of interest in sex. Here are a few of the most common:

1. *Just being that way.* For whatever reason, some people simply never seem to muster much energy for sex-related in-

terests. Typically, their level of sexual activity reflects their lack of interest, although some people manage to live up to external standards by being sexually active even though they don't care much about it. A part of understanding our own sexual individuality often is becoming comfortable with what seems to be our built-in energy level for sexual matters, regardless of where that level may be.

2. *Discouragement with unsatisfying sex.* Many people gradually lose interest in sex after a period of time when their sexual lives have in some way been unsatisfying. For men with continuing erectile or ejaculation problems, or women who don't find real pleasure in sex, the desire even to bother with sex often begins to fade. Eventually, sexual interests get left farther and farther behind as the individual avoids the area of life that has been so troublesome. It is easy to get out of a habit when it continually generates negative feelings.

3. *Placing a low priority on sex.* At various times in their lives, many people take sex for granted. They know it will be there when they want it, and other activities become more pressing. Often without fully realizing it, people shift their sexual feelings into a lower-level priority. It just doesn't matter much anymore. For those who have been troubled by sex, this development is a relief, but for those who suddenly begin wondering what happened to their sex lives, it can be scary.

4. *The attitudes we've learned.* Chuck grew up with negative attitudes toward sex. He was taught that the less he said, felt, and did about sex, the better. He found other interests to occupy his mind and avoided sexual matters as much as possible. Whenever he experienced sexual interests or arousal, he felt dirty and guilty. Obviously, built-in negative attitudes can play an important part in the choice that some people make not to allow themselves much interest in sex. Just how we learn to interpret the things we see also may play a part. Some people see everything through sex-colored glasses, interpreting every word or gesture as a sexual proposition. Amy didn't see things

this way, and her friends had accused her of being cold sexually. "I like sex," she said to me, "but I don't get turned on every time somebody looks at me, or every time I touch a guy. Sex is a very special part of my life that I like to save for special people and occasions. I'm not about to fake some overpowering interest in sex that I don't even feel." Amy was one of those people who understood herself very well and kept sex in a perspective that was comfortable for her.

Finding your potential

The important thing is to find the level of sexual interest that seems to fit you best. That must mean being careful about adopting others' standards as your own, a surefire way of creating sexual worries and problems. If *you* are upset about seeing your sexual interests sag too low, there is one important thing to keep in mind: *your sexual potential is always there.* Much of the old fire can be rekindled if you establish the proper conditions for yourself. You may *choose* the level of interest that suits you best, and the exercises that follow can help.

Where are you—where do you want to be?

Before doing this questionnaire, you should carefully evaluate your reasons for being concerned about a low level of sexual interest. Make sure the concern is yours, and not the invention of someone who feels you're not living up to his expectations. Also, if your sinking interest in sex seems to result from difficulties in the relationship between you and your partner, or from continuing sexual problems of other sorts, work on those aspects of your life first. Other chapters of this book may help, or you may want to consider consulting a professional counselor or sex therapist.

1. *Where are you?* Read through the following statements and decide which of them describe you and your situation. Check those that apply to you:

——————   I have never been as interested in sex as most others seem to be.

_____ I used to be more interested in sex, but recently I have had a more "take it or leave it" attitude.

_____ I don't really see what other people see in sex.

_____ I generally spend very little time thinking about sex.

_____ I rarely am interested in talking about sex with others.

_____ When there is a choice in books and movies, I tend to choose those that do not have sexy themes.

_____ It is seldom that I feel like participating in sexual activity.

_____ My daydreams and fantasies seldom have much to do with sex.

Now look back at the number of check marks you have made. Ask yourself: *so what*? Do you really want to change? If so, why? Maybe you will discover that you do not have as low a sexual interest as you thought. The next exercise may help you determine the level of sexual interest you would like to develop.

2. *Where do you want to be?* Following are some scales with which to rate yourself. On each scale rate yourself by making two marks:

N = Where you think you are now
P = Where you would prefer to be

1	2	3	4	5
Never feel interested in sex		Sometimes interested in sex		Feel interested in sex most of the time

1	2	3	4	5
Never think about sex		Occasionally think about sex		Usually think about sex

1	2	3	4	5
Never feel as if I am "sexy" to others		Sometimes feel as if I am "sexy" to others		Usually feel as if I am "sexy" to others

1	2	3	4	5
Never suggest to a partner that we have sex		Occasionally suggest to a partner that we have sex		Often suggest to a partner that we have sex

1	2	3	4	5
Never have time or energy for sex		Sometimes feel like sex; sometimes not		Always ready to give sex some time and energy

1	2	3	4	5
Feel as if sex does not have any importance in my life		Feel as if sex has only medium importance in my life		Feel as if sex is highly important in my life

These scales are simply a way for you to see the ways in which you would like to change, if any. The suggestions that follow may help.

Developing your sexual interests

When men consult me about sagging sexual interests, and we decide together that it is an area of their lives in need of change, there are three areas on which I ask them to work:

1. *Thinking patterns.* You are what you think. If you *think* your interest in sex is fading, it will surely fade. It is also possible to get back on the track of recognizing your sexual potentials.

2. *Priorities.* The lower the priority you put on sex, the less importance it will hold in your life. In order to change any aspect of your life you must *choose* to place a higher priority on it. You can help sexual interests to become more of a habit if you want to.

3. *Sexual response.* One of the ways in which your level of interest in sex is reflected is the sexual responsiveness of your body. It is possible to pay more attention to your sexual body sensations and to the responsiveness of your sex organs through the use of some simple exercises.

Thinking sexy

A starting point for increasing your sexual interests is to set aside some time for *thinking* about sex. Here are some suggestions:

1. Make an effort to take ten to twenty minutes out of your daily schedule purposely to think about sex. Decide ahead of time what aspects of sex you want to think about. You might want to dwell on your goals for becoming more sexy, or think about sexual activities you would enjoy. Find the sex-related thoughts that interest you most.

2. Choose a sexy novel or a factual book about human sexuality and read it over a period of several days. Or buy a popular magazine that carries sexy pictures and articles about sex to look at and read.

3. Try a few sexual fantasies. Let your imagination go to work on inventing some wild sexual adventures in your head. If you feel turned on by the fantasies, you are giving your sexual interest levels a boost.

4. Ask somebody you trust to talk about sex with you. Be careful the other person doesn't misinterpret your intentions. Seek out a sex educator or sex counselor, if you wish, who can answer questions you might have about sex.

5. If you have lost interest over a period of time, try to re-

member the things that used to interest you about sex. Think about them in detail; maybe you will find them interesting all over again.

Developing a habit

One of the most important ways to develop your sexual interests is by placing a higher priority on sex in your life. In other words, you make it more of a habit instead of taking it for granted. Here is a guide for placing a higher priority on sex in your life:

> How often do you save time for any type of sexual activity during a typical week? ———— times
>
> How long a period of time would you spend in the activity (including all experiences from start to finish) on the average? ———— minutes

Now decide to increase the amount of time you spend with sex. Set some goals for yourself and make a contract with yourself to meet these goals:

> I will increase the number of times I experience sexual activity to ———— times per week, providing this meets with the approval of any partner who might be involved.
>
> I will increase the amount of time spent in my typical sexual activities so that I will spend *no less than* ———— minutes each time.

Reminders for your body

Finally, a good way to maintain or increase your interest in sex is to feel sexual arousal in your body. You need to take the time to generate and enjoy the sensations of being turned on sexually. For men, I suggest the following exercise to encourage them to place a higher priority on feeling sexy.

Each day, at a time when you would not typically feel very interested in sex, take some time out in a private place where you will not be interrupted. Touch your penis and scrotum.

Give yourself an erection if you can do so without difficulty. Take a few minutes to get your body sexually aroused, but do *not* reach an orgasm. Just enjoy the feeling of being turned on and then go on with your daily activities. This exercise tends to develop your awareness of sexual feelings and increase your longing for the pleasurable satisfaction of orgasm. Savor that feeling and save it for later. Look forward to your next sexual experience.

BODY PROBLEMS AND SEX

Any time you are physically ill, your interest in sex may be temporarily lost or reduced. Any condition that produces pain can interfere with the ability to relax and enjoy sex. Some diseases that affect the kidneys or liver may decrease sexual interests and abilities. Disorders of the nervous system, such as multiple sclerosis or Parkinson's disease, may interfere with sexual functioning. There are other physical problems that can affect the male sex organs more directly and change a man's sex life considerably. Most of them require medical treatment by a qualified physician.

Problems of the penis and surrounding area

Men generally don't have many problems with their penises, but there are a few things that can interfere with sex. Some men worry about a *curving of the penis*, which is particularly evident when their penises are erect. Usually, such a curvature results from the way the penis is worn in the underwear over the years and is nothing to worry about. Sometimes, especially in older men, a condition develops called Peyronie's disease, which involves the accumulation of fibrous tissue in the spongy inner chambers of the penis. In a small percentage of males with Peyronie's disease, calcium is deposited in this fibrous tissue, leading to a hardening of the inner parts of the penis and a curving of the organ sideways or upward. In these cases, erection becomes painful and sexual activity involving the penis may become impossible.

It is a good idea to be somewhat cautious when your penis is fully erect. Injury to the erect penis may rip some of the inner tissues. Although such tears may often be treated, they sometimes lead to a permanent weakening in the penis wall, which results in uncomfortable and inconvenient bending during sexual acts.

There is a variety of diseases and irritants that can cause the penis to become suddenly and painfully erect, without the man feeling any sexual desire. This condition is called *priapism*. It may sound like an ideal thing to happen but is generally so uncomfortable that sex is impossible. Serious damage to the penis may result if the unwanted erection remains for more than a day or two. The capability of erection may be permanently lost. Priapism sometimes occurs after the use of so-called aphrodisiacs, such as "Spanish fly," which causes irritation of the penile blood vessels.

Some uncircumcised males have an unusually long or tight foreskin that cannot be easily pulled back over the head of the penis. This condition is called *phimosis* and may interfere with erection and sexual encounters in which the man would like to use his penis. Another complication of phimosis is the accumulation of secretions on the head of the penis, which may lead to infections or sores.

Men often worry and wonder about the possibility of cancer of the penis, but this is rare. Some earlier research suggested that penile cancer is more common in uncircumcised men, but recent studies have questioned that conclusion.

More common than these specific penis problems are annoying infections of the area surrounding the penis. Two typical problems are *jock itch* and *crabs*. Neither of them directly interferes with sex, but they may make you an undesirable sexual partner and create enough itching to be more than a little annoying. Jock itch is caused by a fungus, so the best way to prevent it is by not giving the fungus the right conditions for growing in your crotch. This means avoiding overly tight clothing, drying your genitals thoroughly after a shower, washing well after sweaty activity, and perhaps using some talcum or baby powder. If you get stuck with jock itch anyway, there are several medications available at drugstores which will help. Crabs, or pubic lice, are usually caught directly from a sexual partner, although you can get them from the sheets or clothing of an infected person. You may be able to see the lice in your pubic hair, or a brownish discoloration may appear on the skin, and there is always plenty of itching. Medications that kill crabs (such as Kwell) are usually only available with a doctor's prescription.

There are several medical problems that can affect the testes, although they rarely have much effect on men's sex lives. Before a male is born, both testes are supposed to descend from inside the abdomen down into the scrotal sac. Occasionally, one or both of the testes fail to descend and must be treated medically. This is usually done in childhood. Fluid may sometimes build up in the scrotum, or the testes themselves may swell. As with any physical disorder, unusual or painful developments in the scrotum should be checked out by a physician.

Prostate problems

For men, the inner sex organ most prone to difficulty is the *prostate gland*. In many males the prostate gradually enlarges after they have passed middle age. The most common effect of this enlargement is a slowing down of urine flow from the penis, but unless the prostate becomes exceptionally enlarged, it does not interfere with sexual functioning. In a small percentage of men, enlargement of the prostate is caused by a malignant tumor. *Prostatic cancer* often has no symptoms until it has spread dangerously to other parts of the body. Among men over fifty, prostate cancer claims more lives than any other type of malignancy.

There is a simple procedure by which a physician may check your prostate for signs of enlargement or tumors. It should be done annually in adult men. The doctor, wearing a rubber glove and lubricating one finger, will insert a finger into your rectum.

Typically, the physician will ask you to bend over and bear down as if you were going to have a bowel movement (you won't). It is easy for the doctor to feel the prostate gland through the rectal wall. This procedure is a little uncomfortable and places you in a somewhat humble posture, but is an important way to prevent the serious consequences of prostatic cancer. When caught early, it can usually be completely eliminated through surgery. Your surgeon can inform you about the aftereffects of prostate surgery, which do not in any way reduce the enjoyment of sex.

A more common problem, and one that you are quite likely to face at some point in your life, is *prostatitis*, or inflammation of the prostate gland. A variety of bacteria and viruses may infect the prostate. Sexual irregularity or a sudden change in the frequency of sexual activity may cause *congestive prostatitis*. One of my clients, who was comparatively inactive sexually, wanted to improve his ejaculatory control. He did the self-help exercises rapidly and began ejaculating every day. Unfortunately, his prostate wasn't quite up to all this stimulation, and he began to have cramping sensations in his pelvic area. A two-day break relieved his symptoms. Likewise, the man who has frequent orgasms and suddenly cuts back on sexual activity may experience the discomfort of the buildup of secretions in a prostate gland that is used to getting rid of its fluids on a more regular basis. The best prevention for congestive prostatitis is to avoid sudden changes in your frequency of sexual arousal.

If you get prostatitis from a bacterial or viral infection, you will probably first feel some degree of pain in the pelvic area, typically along the rectum or urinary canal. You may feel the discomfort only when urinating or having a bowel movement. If the infection worsens, you may feel generally run-down and experience nausea or diarrhea. There may be some pus discharged from your penis, and erections or ejaculations may become painful.

If you get any of these symptoms, your first step should be to visit the doctor, who may prescribe an antibiotic for you.

While trying to clear up a bout with prostatitis, there are several other things you may want to try. Good hot baths often help to relieve pain and reduce swelling, as may sitting on a heating pad. It is wise to avoid spicy foods and alcohol, because they tend to lead to irritation of the prostate during urination.

Unfortunately, a good share of men develop chronic prostatitis, meaning that it continues for a long time and may recur whenever the man is tired or run-down.

One of the most startling things that can happen to a man during sex is to have an orgasm without the appearance of semen—a *dry ejaculation*. Some men mistakenly call this "impotence." There are two medical reasons for this. In some cases the body simply doesn't produce the fluids that form the semen, so when orgasm occurs, there is nothing to come out of the penis. The other reason for dry ejacuation is when the semen gets rerouted and is ejaculated up into the urinary bladder instead of through the penis. In medicine this is called *retrograde ejaculation*. Although it may be bothersome, retrograde ejaculation does not cause any damage to the body.

There are several tranquilizers that sometimes produce dry ejaculation in men who take them. If you experience the problem while taking any sort of tranquilizer (such as Thorazine, Mellaril, or Stelazine), find out from your doctor if your difficulties can be attributed to the medication. If so, your ejaculations will return after you cease using the drug. If the lack of ejaculation is bothering you, the physician might be able to prescribe a medication that will not have this annoying side effect.

Men who have had prostate surgery (see also page 164) may also experience dry ejaculation when they begin having sex again. Unfortunately, not all surgeons inform prostate patients ahead of time that loss of ejaculation is a possible consequence of the surgery, so some men are surprised and alarmed to lose this part of their sex lives. So far, medicine hasn't been able to do much about dry ejaculations resulting from prostate operations. Most men find that after a period of time they adjust to the lack of semen and learn to enjoy the pleasure of orgasm without ejaculation. In fact, some appreciate that they no longer must worry about birth control.

Not much is known about *unsatisfying ejaculation*. This involves an oozing out of semen at the time of ejaculation without any of the pleasurable contractions that normally accompany orgasm. It is fairly common for a man to experience an occasional ejaculation that doesn't feel all that great. Any irritation or infection of the prostate or urinary tract may reduce the pleasure of ejaculation temporarily. But sometimes a man finds that each time he has sex, his orgasms are accompanied by a dribbling out of semen and none of the pulsing contractions that used to feel so good. Any time you have continuing difficulty with unsatisfying ejaculation, see your doctor for an evaluation of the cause.

VD or not VD?

There are many sources of information about venereal diseases and other diseases that may be transmitted through sexual contact, so this section will be brief. The most important point to make is that VD is dangerous. You must have it treated and take the responsibility of not spreading it to others. You should also notify the person who gave it to you and anyone you might have given it to, so that they can seek medical treatment.

Within about a week after sexual contact, if you begin to experience pain or burning when you urinate, or an annoying itching sensation in your urethra, and if pus is being discharged through your penis, you may have *gonorrhea* ("clap," "the drip"). You may also have a nonvenereal infection of the urethra that can be caused by loads of different bacteria, viruses, and parasites. These are usually caught from a sexual partner but may sometimes come from other sources. Regardless of the cause, *don't take any chances*. If you let the infection go without proper medical treatment, the troublesome symptoms will eventually disappear, but the germs are probably farther into your body and inner sexual organs. Painful and dangerous infections of your testes, prostate, bladder, or kidneys may result. Untreated gonorrhea may also lead to serious problems, such as sterility, arthritis, heart disease, and meningitis. Only medical laboratory tests can show whether or not your symptoms are caused by gonorrhea. If they are, prompt treatment with penicillin or another antibiotic is almost always fully effective.

Syphilis in males usually begins with the appearance of a painless, oozing sore (called a chancre) on or near the penis, within a month and a half after the sexual contact. Occasionally, the chancre appears in the mouth or anal region if that is where sexual activity has occurred. Of course, pimples, warts, and other sores can occur on the penis, and men often worry about any sort of blemish in the genital area. It is always a good idea to check out the possibility of syphilis if there is any chance you may have been exposed. If syphilis is not treated with antibiotics, the chancre will eventually heal and the disease germs move farther into the body to do more serious damage. Untreated, the disease can drag on for years and attack any of the body's inner organs.

There are other venereal diseases that are less common than gonorrhea and syphilis, both of which have again reached epidemic proportions. One of the other forms of VD that has been on the increase in recent years is the *herpesvirus 2*. It is a particularly troublesome disease because there are no known treatments that will kill viruses. In a man who has been infected with herpes 2, small, painful blisters appear on the sex organs. The blisters eventually rupture to form soft, painful, open sores. These sores will heal, but the virus continues to inhabit the man's body and the blisters may appear at any time, especially when he is physically run-down and more susceptible. The disease is highly contagious and may have serious consequences for others. Women who get herpes 2 are more susceptible to uterine cancer. Babies who become infected at birth may have serious illnesses.

For centuries, VD was seen as the punishment for engaging in sinful sex. When medicine discovered the "miracle drugs" to treat these diseases, many people stopped worrying about them. That is one reason why VD has increased so much in recent years. Prevention and treatment of VD is one of the responsibilities that accompanies the pleasures of sex.

Surmounting greater obstacles

There are more serious medical problems that some men have to face when trying to establish a meaningful sexual life. Although such conditions are rare, some male babies are born with abnormalities of the penis. Sometimes the penis has not formed properly, leaving it open along the upper or lower surface. Surgical repair is necessary in these cases, but the surgery may leave malformations that interfere with normal erection and ejaculation. Yet even these obstacles may be overcome.

One young man who sought counseling from me had been born with a condition requiring extensive surgery on his urinary bladder and penis. His sex organ was left partly attached to his body so that it could not stand outward during erection. Semen was ejaculated from an opening in his body at the base of his penis and on the underside. He knew that he would never be able to have sexual intercourse in the same manner as most men but was very attracted to women and very determined to share an active sex life. Through effective communication involving a great deal of honesty about his feelings, he was able to work out pleasurable sexual encounters with several partners over a period of years. Eventually, he married one of these women, and they were even able to achieve pregnancy.

Spinal injuries and strokes may lead to paralysis in the pelvic area, and many people mistakenly assume that a paralyzed man cannot respond sexually. In reality, many males who are paralyzed still can achieve erection and ejaculation. Rehabilitation programs for spinal injury victims are now helping men find new and effective ways of continuing to lead happy sex lives with their partners.

Sexual feelings and needs can remain despite physical handicaps. How they are expressed in sexual activity is only as limited as a man's imagination.

KEEPING IN SHAPE FOR SEX

Sex involves the total body, and sexual functioning may be influenced by physical fitness, nutritional balance, and chemical substances in the body. The individual who is run-down, out of shape, not eating properly, or overindulging in alcohol or other drugs will usually begin to see an effect on his or her sex life.

Unfortunately, not much reliable, scientifically researched information is available concerning the effects of these factors on sex. I am going to provide you with some common sense approaches to keeping in shape for sex, based on my observations of men in sex therapy and people in general. The most important point to make here is that none of these suggestions will give you overnight results. As with anything that affects our bodies, noticeable results show up only after several weeks of *consistent* use.

Being sexy with what you eat

For centuries, people have been searching for quick-acting love potions. Many foods have been given reputations along the way as instant turn-ons. Everything from olives and eggs to bananas and peanut butter has been recommended. Most nutritionists and sexologists agree that whatever effects these foods have on your sex life, they are determined by your head. It's an old story—if you think it's going to work, it does. I don't know of any food or chemical that actually has a direct effect on the improvement of sexual functioning.

However, I am convinced that good nutrition is important to good health and that a healthy body will typically make sex more enjoyable. One of the measures for determining the effectiveness of your diet is your waistline. Carrying too many pounds not only affects your health but makes you feel unattractive. Both results can easily affect sex. If you are over-weight, you haven't been eating, or probably exercising, properly. Men particularly get into habits of grabbing meaty, greasy foods and wolfing them down in a hurry. These habits are dangerous over the long run.

Nutrition has a direct effect on our glands and nervous systems, both of which play a major role in sexual activity. Several of the major sex researchers, including Alfred Kinsey, have noted that there is a link between nutrition and the frequency of human sexual behaviors.

SOME SAFE RULES FOR EATING SEXY

1. Eat a well-balanced diet, which includes a selection of carbohydrates, proteins, and fats daily.

2. When trying to lose weight, avoid "crash" or fad diets, especially those that do not provide a balance of different foods. Consult a qualified nutritionist, or physician who understands nutrition, for proper guidance in calorie management, and set a sensible goal of losing just a few pounds each week or month.

3. Avoid overindulging in foods with high sugar content.

4. Be cautious about fatty foods and oils unless you get plenty of exercise each day.

5. Drink plenty of water. Your urine should be nearly clear at least once a day. If it is dark or cloudy, you may not be getting enough liquids.

6. Eat lots of fresh fruits, vegetables, grains, and other fibers. More and more evidence is pointing to the importance of fiber in the diet.

7. Consider taking supplementary vitamins. Although there is plenty of debate about vitamins, it is likely that extra amounts of vitamins B, C, and E are beneficial to sexual health.

8. Experimenting with some respected "health foods" won't hurt either, if you choose to do so. They should be made

a part of your daily diet and not be "extras." Otherwise you'll be overeating. Some foods worth trying are wheat germ and wheat germ oil, honey, and *raw* nuts and seeds (such as sesame or pumpkin). If you are even more adventurous, you might want to experiment with kelp (a type of seaweed that you can buy processed) and cod-liver oil (in capsules). Don't expect miracles; give them time to work.

Alcohol, drugs, and your sex life

Drugs can knock out your sexual interests or increase them. They can also knock out a man's sexual responses, including erection and ejaculation. Most chemical substances tend to interfere with sexual pleasure rather than improve it.

Alcohol and other depressant drugs, in lesser amounts, reduce fear and anxiety and help people to relax. Since relaxation is such an important part of successful sex, the sexual experience may be improved. Problems arise when the level of alcohol or drugs in the body increases to a point where it begins to interfere with sexual function. For a man, this may mean erection problems, delayed orgasm, or other problems with ejaculation.

The effects of marijuana seem to vary in different individuals and in different circumstances. It sometimes is relaxing and creates a greater awareness of sexual feelings. Some marijuana users report that the drug intensifies their awareness of sexual feeling so much that the reactions become unpleasant.

Amphetamines, cocaine, LSD, and a variety of other chemical substances are reported by some users to improve sex, but medical evidence suggests that habitual use or heavy doses of any of them are likely to interfere with sex and of course are risks to health. Amyl nitrite, a medication used for patients with heart trouble, is claimed to intensify orgasm if popped at the peak of sexual arousal. However, it too may be dangerous, as there are cases of fatal heart attacks following the use of amyl nitrite during intercourse.

I always caution my clients in therapy against allowing chemical substances to become *necessary* to their enjoyment of sex. Nothing can spoil sex more quickly than having always to rely on an outside substance for kicks. For most people, tuning in to the body's reactions and feeling the sensations of the skin and sex organs can probably duplicate nearly any amount of extra enjoyment a drug might provide.

Body fitness and sex

Our society gives us plenty of opportunity to get out of shape and stay that way—too much food, too much pressure, not enough rest, and too little exercise. The average man may lack the stamina to run a couple of hundred yards without gasping for breath, but most men have the endurance to last through a reasonably strenuous sexual encounter. Nevertheless, if you're out of shape, you don't feel as sexy, enjoy your body so much, or have the same amount of energy left for sex after a busy day as someone who is in shape.

Physical activity is constantly needed to condition the muscles, heart, and entire circulatory system. Without exercise, the body's balances are disrupted. Weight, blood pressure, heart rate, and fat levels in the blood all go up, while oxygen consumption, flexibility, efficiency, strength, stamina, and probably sexual interests decrease.

The more exercise you get as long as you are in good health and don't exhaust yourself, the better. The first step must be your decision to get involved. You may not see noticeable effects on your sex life right away, but it is likely that in time you will.

To achieve and maintain physical fitness, you need exercise that gets your heart pumping faster and speeds up your breathing. Weight lifting and isometric exercises are fine for building muscles, but experts usually recommend running, bicycling, or swimming as ideal forms of conditioning exercise. Other possibilities—such as jumping rope—tend to be more dull.

If you're ready to get in shape, get a book on exercise and get started. The results will show up before long, and you will be living a happier, healthier life.

7

Making It Together

In my experience with couples, I have found that one of the major difficulties is the *expectations* with which two people start a relationship. A young married couple came into my office several months ago, certain that their partnership was headed for disaster. "I know this sounds really corny," the wife said, "but it seems as if the spark has gone out of our marriage. We're in a rut that neither one of us seems able to get out of. We don't even care about having sex anymore." Her husband agreed and couldn't understand where things had gone sour. I asked them to talk about the kinds of expectations they had originally set for each other and their marriage. They were typical:

> We'll always feel excitedly in love with one another.
>
> Our sex life will always be fresh and exciting.
>
> It's always going to be fun to be together.
>
> As long as we share a good sex life, we should never feel sexually attracted to anyone else.
>
> Once we get settled into this relationship, all of our problems will be small ones.

We'll always be able to talk things out calmly and reasonably.

Our sexual likes and dislikes will always be the same.

These statements are filled with expectations for always and ever after by which most people can never live. For people who enter a loving relationship, the love changes over a period of time. Things don't have to get worse, but they do change. In the early stages of loving, people are filled with a desire to be with the loved one, to get more and more intimate. There is a thrill to the sight, touch, and smell of one another. Eventually, two people go about as far as they can in getting close to each other. They stop "falling in love." That is when most couples panic and the point at which many relationships end. It feels as if "it just isn't there anymore."

When you've stopped falling in love, it doesn't have to mean that things are over. It may just mean you're ready to enjoy *being in love*. That means a mutual sense of caring, closeness, trust, and respect. At times you may also feel bored or angry with each other or get sick of being together for brief periods. But you both know the love and commitment that are there, and every so often you feel real surges of love that are like falling in love all over again.

The same sort of process often happens in a couple's sex life. At first, there are new highs, different positions, activities yet to be tried. But for most couples there is a sense of boredom that sets in with the same old sexual routines. It may also be scary when you find yourself, or your partner, sexually attracted to someone else. Surprisingly, many men and women believe that when you have a happy, satisfying sex life, you shouldn't find people other than your partner attractive and interesting. Actually most people who are involved in committed, lasting relationships still enjoy looking at and fantasizing about others. Human beings do not necessarily have the same sexual tastes for a lifetime either. New possibilities may become interesting, and old partners may be left behind, all a part of a changing, growing partnership.

One thing is extremely important to keep in mind. Problems can come up in any partnership involving a shared sexual life together. Yet, by knowing how to communicate about and work on sexual problems, you may find improved—even more exciting—ways of enjoying sex together.

The best way to keep your sex life together interesting is to keep in touch with your partner's expectations, as well as your own—and don't set unrealistic goals.

The greening of sex—jealousy

Dave and Cindy had been involved in a loving relationship for about two years, and their sex life seemed satisfactory for both of them. I first saw them after some trouble began to develop. Cindy explained their feelings. "Dave and I don't believe that love should be a trap. If we love each other, it means that both of us are free to grow in our own directions and that each of us will find joy whenever the other is happy. A long time ago we decided we wanted a completely open relationship. Dave and I would be the central and most important partnership, but each of us would be free to have friendships, love, and sex with other people. The meaning of sex is exaggerated, and we think it can be shared with other people even if you're involved in a close primary relationship."

The only problem was that Cindy and Dave's philosophy wasn't working for them in practice. When one of them was with someone else, the other felt worried and depressed, wondering all the time what was going on. They both had sex with other partners, and they had agreed to be honest with each other about it. Dave found himself asking Cindy very specific questions about what she did with other men. When she told him, he would get upset but still keep questioning her for more information. As she realized how much her answers were bothering him, she would get angry at his questions and accuse him of being insecure about his masculinity. "What's the matter," she sometimes said, "do you think I'm going to find somebody who's better in bed?"

The situation had been going around in circles for several

months before I saw them in my office. They were bewildered and discouraged. "Some days I think I have everything under control and feel very close to Cindy," said Dave. "Then the next day I may be resentful and disgusted. One minute I can feel like marrying her, and the next I want to break up." Both of them had begun to doubt their love and the meaning of sex in their relationship.

The crux of their difficulty was their attitude toward the jealousy they were both feeling so intensely. Dave put it this way: "Jealousy is just a way of saying you don't really trust the strength of your love together. It's a sign of insecurity." Cindy put it even more bluntly: "Jealousy is sick."

Another man I know said that jealousy is a sign of ownership, adding, "You can't own other people. You have to let the people you love be free to find whatever sexual fulfillment they can—with you or without you. If you can't take it, then maybe you don't love them as much as you'd like to think."

Many couples struggle with the problem of jealousy in their sex lives. They vary from partners who have decided anything goes sexually, to those who get insulted and angry if their partners even glance at anyone else. Most of us fit somewhere in between.

The real key to sexual happiness together is for both of you to feel comfortable not only with your philosophies and plans for the ideal relationship, but also with the way you feel on a day-to-day basis. If you feel anger, resentment, hurt, or that elusive emotion we call *jealousy*, something is wrong and not necessarily with you. There are those counselors and psychologists who believe jealousy to be a sign of insecurity and lack of trust, and surely it sometimes is. Other professionals, however, view jealousy as a natural human reaction to having your "territory" violated. Although you can never "own" another human being, you can become quite dependent on her or him and want to save aspects of your relationship together as special things only the two of you will share. In many cases, the most special thing is sex.

There are no black-and-white answers here. Some couples

get along very nicely with sexually open relationships (although they often have to work more than they expect on the problems that arise). Other couples are happier agreeing not to share sex outside the relationship (the danger here comes if one partner "cheats" on the agreement).

Finding your way around sexual jealousy

The best way to avoid jealousy in your sex life is to *prevent* it before it happens. Here are some suggestions for accomplishing that:

1. *Think over your sexual values.* Spend time honestly thinking through what your sexual beliefs and needs are. The idea of being free to have sex any time you want, and with anyone, is appealing to a lot of us. But think carefully about how much you would really want this freedom and how much you'd like your partner to have the same freedom.

2. *Talk with your partner about what you want and expect from each other.* The most complicated situations arise when one person's sexual expectations are very different from the other's. In such cases you might even have to make the difficult decision of whether or not the differences are important enough to mean that your relationship cannot be successful. Not all couples can find a middle ground for being happy together. A counselor may be able to help you sort through these issues.

3. *Be willing to "test the waters."* No matter what kind of agreement you and your partner come to, test it out cautiously to see if it works in real life. Lots of things seem good and right until they are put into practice. Be prepared for unexpected results and think ahead to different possible courses of action. No matter what you have decided together, be open to change.

4. *Listen to your feelings.* Don't just analyze with your head. Your feelings have lots of things to tell you as well. If something doesn't seem to sit just right inside, admit it, deal with it, talk about it together.

Sometimes unreasonable jealousy develops, and this can seriously endanger a relationship. Murray never thought much of himself and was amazed when Karen fell in love with him. His own insecurity and low feelings of self-worth kept getting in the way, however. He was always afraid of losing her and became upset every time she talked with another man. Karen constantly felt trapped and "possessed" by Murray, and this was gradually pushing them apart until Murray began to work on his unreasonable jealousy.

If you feel that you need to work on your own insistent feelings of unreasonable jealousy, here are some suggestions:

1. *Accept your jealousy.* It's nothing to be ashamed of. You are afraid of losing your partner, and that is scary. It is particularly difficult when you know your partner is attracted to someone else, even though that doesn't necessarily mean that she or he is rejecting you. But let yourself feel all you need to feel and communicate it to your partner.

2. *Work on finding your own wholeness and independence.* Even partners who enjoy spending a lot of time together need time apart. Both people in a partnership must feel good about themselves, and feel worthwhile and useful, when they are not together.

3. *Realize that you cannot always be first and that you cannot fill all of your partner's needs.* Your partner may seek companionship and sharing with other people too. That is not any reflection on your worth or importance to her or him. It simply is true that you cannot fulfill *all* of another's needs. You can't be everything all of the time, nor should you be. You are not solely responsible for your partner's happiness and well-being, nor is she or he for yours.

4. *Remember that you are only as trapped as you allow yourself to be.* You can make changes in your life and in your relationship, if you choose to do so. Change can be difficult, but it may also help us grow.

I have seen many couples go through the agonies of jealousy. It is not at all unusual for people to have sex outside their partnerships, and their relationships are often thrown into turmoil by the jealousy that follows. Some couples break up; others may choose to stay together but lose faith in each other from that time on. Still others are strengthened by the need to work on jealousy together and come to a new level of understanding and a clearer commitment to the kind of sexual life-style that suits them best.

Helping a partner with a sexual problem

The majority of partnerships eventually experience some sex-related problem. Sometimes these difficulties clear up on their own, with little or no attention, but they also can turn into long-term problems that interfere with a couple's sex life for months or even years. It is not at all unusual for couples who have been together for years, and then begin to have sexual trouble, to give up on sex after a while. They may write it off to their age or any other handy excuse that saves them from having to face and deal with the problem.

Exactly how you can help a partner work on her or his sexual problem will depend largely on your personalities and the quality of your relationship. Here are suggestions that could give you some guidelines, however:

1. *Ask yourself what help you would want.* Many times, the ways to help other people lie within ourselves. When your partner is encountering some problem with sex, ask yourself to imagine what it would be like to be in the other person's shoes. How would you feel? What would you want from someone trying to help? How much would you need to feel cared for and worthwhile?

2. *Help take the pressure off.* When you are concerned about a sexual problem, the last thing you want to do is to have to "perform" by having sex. Usually it's a big relief simply to be told that there is no need to have sex until you've

made progress in solving the problem and again feel ready for sex. You want to let your partner know that having sex is important to you, but that you can provide the time to work on the difficulty. As this book demonstrates, working on sexual improvement exercises takes time, and there should be a gradual progression toward more intensively sexual activity. Each of you should have time to relax with and enjoy every step. Taking the pressure off will usually go a long way toward improving your sex life together.

3. *Find sources of information.* There are plenty of books on sex and sexual problems (see the book list on page 235). Both of you will want to become better informed about your partner's sexual problem and what can be done about it. Your willingness to help with this educational process will further express your caring and desire to make things better.

4. *Help your partner find the time to work on the problem.* Many times, when someone is troubled by sex, it is an easy part of life to push into the background and avoid. Without creating undue pressure, it may be important for you to work with your partner in scheduling time together for sexual exercises. Don't push and don't be inflexible, but demonstrate your sincere interest in dealing with the problem.

5. *Know your limits.* You may be too close to the situation, and you might even be part of the problem. Beyond a certain point, there is nothing you can do to help your partner out of a sexual worry. That may be the point at which you both will want to seek some outside professional help, as discussed later in this chapter. Know your limits and don't expect that you can necessarily be your partner's sexual savior.

TAKING STOCK: YOUR RELATIONSHIP AND SEX

This questionnaire is designed to help you and your partner evaluate some aspects of the relationship and sexual life that you share together. It poses some important questions that you may never have thought much about or discussed together. You may choose to do the questionnaire alone and think about the results yourself. However, it works best if you and your partner both write down answers to the questions on separate sheets of paper. Then when you are both finished, take about ten or fifteen minutes to read over each other's answers *without* any argument or discussion. The next step is to talk out your findings together, following some of the basic rules of communication found in Chapter 2. Where were your surprise answers? Which of your partner's answers do you disagree with and why? On what issues are the two of you farthest apart, and on which are you closest together? What areas of your relationship need the most work?

1. From the following list, pick those words that best describe *your* present feelings about the overall relationship you are now sharing with your partner (add words of your own if you wish):

satisfied	trapped	secure	jealous
lonely	settled	uncaring	tolerant
contented	unhappy	appreciative	insecure
dissatisfied	loving	disillusioned	joyful
warm	confused	happy	uncertain

2. Now re-examine the preceding list and pick those words you believe would most accurately reflect your partner's feelings toward your relationship, again adding words to the list if you wish.

3. On each of the following issues, rate where you and your partner stand, using this rating scale:

5 = My partner and I are in complete agreement here and happy with our choice.

4 = My partner and I tend to agree on this, although I'm not certain how things would work out if it were tested in real life.

3 = I am uncertain how we feel about this.

2 = My partner and I don't always agree on this, but it hasn't created serious problems.

1 = My partner and I strongly disagree here, and it represents an unresolved conflict for our relationship.

_____ The degree to which you both should be dependent on the relationship and each other.

_____ The amount of freedom you both should have for friendships outside your relationship.

_____ How free you both should be to love other people outside your relationship, without sexual involvement.

_____ How free *you* yourself should be to have sexual relationships with other partners.

_____ How you both would handle a situation in which one of you "cheated" on the other sexually.

_____ How much each of you should "give up" for the other's happiness and security.

_____ How permanent and lasting your relationship will be.

4. On a scale of 1 (awful) to 10 (outstanding), how would you rate the sexual relationship you and your partner presently share? _____

If you rated it a 9 or 10, explain briefly what makes it so good.

If you rated it below a 9, answer the following questions:

a. Do you wish your sexual relationship were better than it is?

b. What factors seem to be interfering with having your sex life be tops?

c. Are these factors bothering or upsetting you?

d. What parts of your sex life seem most in need of work toward improvement?

e. Do you feel that your partner sees things the same way? Where would you guess she/he would rate your sexual relationship?

f. Do you want to work to improve the situation? If so, in what ways are you willing to work?

5. List your partner's best qualities as a sexual mate for you.

6. List what you see as your own best qualities as a sexual mate for your partner.

7. Why is sex important enough to you to be reading this book and trying out this questionnaire?

WOMEN AND THEIR SEXUAL NEEDS

The majority of men who read this book desire women as sexual partners. They enjoy the softness and roundness of women's bodies and love the feeling of being close to female warmth. They get aroused by the thought of sharing an intense sexual encounter with a responsive woman. For years—in books about sex, in novels, and in the movies—we were told that women's sexual needs were very different from those of men. While males were described as the always-horny sexual aggressors, hoping only to get it up, get it in, and get it over with, women were seen as the gentle romantics who enjoyed warm physical closeness more than actual sexual acts. Women have finally broken away from those false roles, as is evidenced by the many new books for women with detailed instructions on how to enjoy sex more. In the past some women did not allow themselves much sexual interest because they had been taught it was unfeminine, and some women are still paying the price in lack of sexual satisfaction.

The fact is that women are as different from one another in their sexual needs and interests as men are. Some women are turned on by romance and slow, loving embraces. Others would rather skip the frills and get down to business. Men differ in the same ways.

Women and touching

There are some common differences between women and men worth mentioning here, however. Women, for example, have often been brought up with very different attitudes toward body touching. It begins in childhood. Boys' sex organs are obvious, and boys handle them a great deal, regardless of how much parents may disapprove. Boys learn very young to hold their penises while urinating. As puberty nears, erections are hard to ignore, and most boys are masturbating to orgasm by the age of twelve or thirteen. Sexual touching is already established as a male way of life.

Girls often pay less attention to their more concealed organs, and there is less practical need to touch them. Somehow society creates an atmosphere that says "nice" little girls just don't do that sort of thing anyway. Females generally start masturbating at later ages and may not try to reach orgasm in doing so. Sexual touching, and enjoyment through it, are much less a part of many females' lives.

This difference sometimes results in sexual difficulties between women and men because the touching aspects of sex have greater importance for some women than they generally do for men. Miriam complained about her husband's urgency with sex: "Just a few strokes and he's ready for intercourse. I like to take my time and be gently touched and massaged until I'm fully turned on. This seems to be boring for him, and I end up feeling most of the time as if he doesn't care much about my body. I don't understand why men are always in such a hurry to get sex over with." Her final complaint reflects the fact that men are sometimes more "orgasm-oriented" than women. They work toward feeling the pleasure of ejaculation, while women usually enjoy savoring the entire sexual experience more.

Not all people fit these patterns, of course. There are women who can't wait for their orgasm, and men who would rather spend an entire night touching and making love without ejaculating. The important thing is for couples to know and understand their differences and work toward a compromise situation that suits them both.

Women's bodies

Frank was about to graduate from college when he appeared in my office. He had had several girl friends during his college years and had experienced intercourse on a few occasions. He thought himself to be sexually inexperienced, however, and was looking for more information. "I've seen plenty of sex books," he explained, "and watched stag movies at my frat house until I'm sick of them, but I still don't feel as if I know much about the female body. A few times when I've been fooling around with women, it has seemed like I did all the right things and touched all the right places, but it was mostly by accident. I've never had a really close look at a woman's sex organs, and no woman has ever bothered to explain what she likes touched the most."

Frank's situation was not unusual, since most men never bother to take steps to learn more about women's bodies. I usually suggest to sexual partners that when they feel ready and comfortable, they spend some time examining each other's sex organs and explaining the importance of their different parts in sexual pleasuring. A labeled diagram or photograph may help you find different sexual parts on one another's bodies.

In some ways a woman's body is not so different from a man's. Her sexual parts are soft and sensitive, and they swell with blood when she is sexually aroused. If you refer to the diagram below, you will be able to pick out the external sex organs that are part of the woman's genital area, or *vulva*.

Under a woman's pubic hair is a mound of tissue called the *mons*. For many women pressure or stroking on the mons is

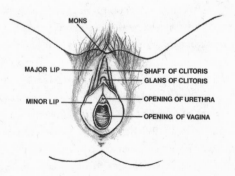

sexually arousing. Two pairs of skin folds cover the main female sex organs. The larger outer folds are the *major lips* (or labia). Their size and shape differ in different women, ranging from thin and rather flat lips to thick, bulging ones. If the major lips are parted, two thinner, irregular folds may be seen inside, the *minor lips* (or labia). Both pairs of lips enlarge somewhat when a woman is sexually aroused, and they may even open slightly.

If you follow the edges of the minor lips toward their tops, you find that they form a hood of tissue covering the *clitoris*. The head, or *glans*, of the clitoris usually protrudes out from under the hood as a small nub, while the clitoral *shaft* extends back under the hood. The clitoris is an especially sensitive organ that responds easily to sexual stimulation. As a woman gets sexually excited, her clitoris becomes erect, filling with blood. The head of the clitoris is particularly sensitive, and prolonged rubbing of its surface often becomes unpleasant. During arousal, the clitoral head retracts under the hood of tissue, apparently to protect it from direct stimulation.

Just beneath the clitoris is the tiny *opening of the urethra*, through which urine leaves a woman's body. It is sometimes difficult to see but may appear as a small pucker. Then beneath the urethra is the opening to the *vagina*. It has an irregular border and may not look much like an opening at all. Actually the vagina is not a hole but a closed canal. The inner walls separate only when something is inserted between them. The vagina has thick, muscular walls, and it is three to four inches deep. It easily expands to accommodate any size penis. During sexual arousal the vaginal walls "sweat," producing a wetness that acts as a lubricant for sexual activity. The outer third of the vagina is the most sensitive part of the organ.

The inner female sex organs have more to do with reproduction. These structures include the uterus, fallopian tubes, and ovaries. Women of childbearing age regularly go through the menstrual cycle. Basically, this prepares the uterus for accepting an embryo. An egg is released from one of the ovaries, and the uterus builds up inner tissues to provide a nurturing surface

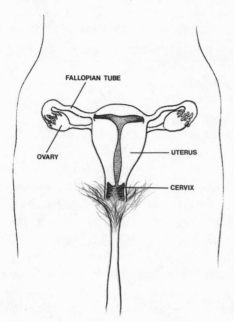

FALLOPIAN TUBE

OVARY

UTERUS

CERVIX

in which a baby could grow. Usually, of course, the egg is not fertilized by a male's sperm, so the extra uterine lining is not needed. It is then shed from the body through the vagina, along with a small amount of blood. This is called menstruation, or the period, and lasts from three to seven days. There is no danger, incidentally, in having sex during the menstrual period; some menstrual fluid may leak out during sex, but this need not create any problems. It is possible for a woman to get pregnant, however, even though she is having her period. The entire menstrual cycle—from the beginning of one period to the beginning of the next—lasts about twenty-eight days on the average, although it may last a longer or shorter time in particular women.

Which parts of her body a woman wants touched during sex varies with the woman, her individual needs, and her partner's skills. Many women find that their breasts are sensitive to touch, and they become easily aroused by breast stimulation. Again, one of the worst mistakes a man can make in sex with a woman is to assume that every woman responds to the same type of stimulation. The best practice is for a man to be open to learning from any sexual partner—to increase the partner's pleasure and his own.

Women's sexual problems

Men and women share some sexual problems. Some women have too-rapid orgasms, just as some men do, but it is rarely considered a problem in women. This is partly because these women may often have more than one orgasm, while a man is typically finished after one. In addition, women can continue having sex even after they have reached orgasm, so a quick orgasm doesn't necessarily signal the end of a sexual experience for the partner.

The two most common functional problems of women are lack of sexual arousal, corresponding to erection problems in the male, and the inability to reach orgasm, similar to the male's delayed ejaculation. A third difficulty, which lacks a male counterpart, is vaginismus, involving a tensing of the outer vaginal muscles. If your female partner is having difficulty with any sexual concerns, you may want to get one of several books now available for women, or consider visiting a sex therapist with her. She will need to work toward these goals with your help, understanding, and cooperation. Let me tell you about three different couples who experienced these problems and what they did about them.

When a woman doesn't get turned on

Kathy and Jason were very discouraged about sex. They had been living together for nearly a year, and their sex life was deteriorating. They had sex several times a week, but Kathy rarely enjoyed it much or felt aroused. Jason had tried everything imaginable but rarely had positive results. Most often, Kathy simply lay there, wishing that the whole experience was over. Jason was getting increasingly frustrated with the situation and often doubted his own sexual adequacy. He sometimes wondered out loud, "I don't understand why I can't get her turned on." More and more, Kathy tried to find excuses to avoid sex altogether.

Situations such as these may be complicated, and sometimes the woman's lack of sexual arousal reflects her lack of satisfaction in the relationship. Partnership counseling is often necessary in these cases. Kathy and Jason wanted to be together, and they both had a sincere interest in improving their sexual enjoyment. Part of the problem was that Kathy had some deep guilt feelings concerning some past sexual experiences about which she had never told Jason. In addition, she always felt hurried in sex and would give up when she thought she just wasn't going to have time to get turned on.

I saw Kathy and Jason over a period of several weeks, prescribing for them a series of sexual exercises that they used at home. Just as in those cases where men experience erection problems, the best place to start is with nonsexual, mutual body pleasuring. The woman is free to enjoy all of the sensations of her body without having to worry about "performing" sexually. She can relax and open herself to any sexual arousal that she feels. Gradually, over a period of weeks, the exercises become more focused on the sex organs, and the couple take their time in allowing the woman to relax and feel comfortable with each new level of accomplishment.

It is extremely important for the man to be understanding and nonpressuring during the process of helping a woman feel her body's sexual responsiveness. The more he is impatient or pushy, the less they will accomplish. It is also important for both partners to keep in mind that different people may have different levels of interest in sex, so you can't always expect to be turned on at exactly the same times your partner is.

Jason and Kathy made good progress with their exercises. One especially good step was taken when Jason realized that he had usually been in too much of a hurry with sex to give Kathy the types of body stimulation she really enjoyed. They discovered this during an exercise in which she guided his hand to do the kinds of things she wanted. Later he said, "It's surprising how many things you take for granted in sex. We never took the time to learn about what we wanted from each other. Now we know." Kathy was responding much more positively to their sexual encounters, although they also began realizing that she was never going to have the degree of interest in sex that Jason had. He explained that this difference was of little consequence to him as long as the times when they did share sex were mutually pleasurable and satisfying.

Things don't always work out as easily as they did for Kathy and Jason, but most women can learn how to relax and be turned on. When the problem lies in more serious problems within the relationship, the situation is usually more difficult to remedy. One woman consulted me about her sexual "problem" after fourteen years of marriage and having four children. Carol explained how she seldom got sexually aroused anymore and that intercourse had become a dreaded event she endured out of a sense of marital duty.

As Carol and I talked further, she revealed that her thirty-eight-year-old husband demanded sex from her at least once, and usually two or three times, a day. Every special occasion or outing had to be "topped off" with intercourse. He would waken her at three or four in the morning to have sex. Bedtime almost always meant intercourse. Carol had attempted at times to refuse his advances, only to be physically forced to submit. She was so saturated with sex, and so bored by its unchanging pattern, that it was no wonder sex had become a dreaded part of her life.

Carol believed herself to be at fault and wanted me to prescribe some way for her to become more interested in sex. Obviously, the difficulty lay in the couple's lack of communication, their differing levels of sexual interest, and the ways in which her needs were being overlooked and ignored by both of them. I attempted to get her husband involved in the counseling process, but he refused, reminding her that the problem was hers. Unhappy as she was, Carol chose to stay in her pressured situation, hoping to find a therapist who would make her into a sexual superwoman capable of responding to all of her husband's hungry sexual needs. Unfortunately, successful outcomes in cases such as these require understanding and cooperation from the woman's sexual partner, and Carol's husband was unwilling to provide these qualities. So she went back to their one-sided sex life, and both of them missed out on what probably could have been a more enjoyable and satisfying way of living together sexually.

Women and orgasm problems

Many women who don't get sexually aroused also never achieve orgasm, although things do not necessarily follow in such a predictable manner. The inability to reach orgasm once she is turned on is a woman's most common sexual complaint. It is frustrating for the woman and often for her partner. However, some women feel satisfied with a sexual encounter without reaching orgasm. If you feel inadequate because your female partner doesn't climax, but she is satisfied, the problem is yours.

Ron and his wife Arlene had faced this problem all of the time during their three-year relationship. She got aroused easily and in their earlier sexual contacts had been eager to share intercourse with Ron. She described her typical response like this: "I get really turned on and enjoy having sex with Ron. I just keep building and building and eventually feel like I must be close to having an orgasm. But I seem to reach a certain level of turn-on, and I just can't come. Then as soon as I realize that I'm not going to make it again, I begin to lose interest, and before we know it, I'm back to ground zero, feeling frustrated and unsatisfied."

A woman may be unable to reach orgasm during intercourse because her male partner ejaculates too soon and the sexual encounter ends. Chapter 4 dealt with the ways in which men can learn better ejaculatory control. This wasn't the difficulty for Arlene and Ron, however. He was able to last about as long as either of them wanted, and she usually had given up on having an orgasm before he was finished.

Arlene was one of those women who had never learned how to experience orgasm. She was somewhat uncomfortable touching her own body, masturbated infrequently, and was unable to give herself an orgasm. They both agreed with my suggestion that Arlene attend a women's group designed for women with orgasm problems. In the several sessions that she attended, she learned several techniques for putting herself in touch with her own body and for providing herself with the necessary stimulation to bring herself to orgasm. At first, Ron felt uncomfortable having Arlene working on the problem without him. It made him feel unnecessary and as if he somehow had let her down. Eventually, he worked through these feelings and realized that it was important for her to know how to enjoy the sexual pleasures of her own body before she could bring her body to him for shared enjoyment. (There are several books available for women that describe these self-help techniques for becoming orgasmic. See the book list on page 236.)

After Arlene had learned to reach orgasm through her own stimulation, I continued to work with the couple. Gradually, they used exercises at home through which Ron learned exactly the kinds of stimulation that she needed to generate orgasm. First she guided his hands and then allowed him to stimulate her on his own. They were eventually able to build what they both learned into their experiences with sexual intercourse, so that she was able to have an orgasm every time.

Not all women with orgasm problems have the degree of difficulty Arlene experienced. Many are able to have orgasm during masturbation, but not during intercourse. Others have trouble climaxing just occasionally. One important thing is becoming clear to sex therapists: sexual intercourse is not the easiest way for many women to reach orgasm. Stimulation of the clitoris is one of the most common ways in which orgasm is generated for females, and intercourse alone does not provide the kind of clitoral touching that may do the trick. Most men have trouble imagining the enjoyment of a sexual encounter in which their penises were not stimulated and did not produce orgasm. For many women with orgasm difficulties, then, it is important that they and their partners learn how to provide some extra clitoral stimulation during intercourse. It is usually not much trouble for one person or the other to slip a hand into position so that fingers can touch the clitoris as intercourse is happening. Every woman has different needs when it comes to the type of clitoral stimulation applied, however, so a man must take his time to learn from his partner exactly what she wants.

Another problem here is with the man who wants his penis to be all things to all partners. It's hard for him to admit that his penis alone simply cannot always do the job. A good male lover knows how to learn from a partner without letting his ego get in the way. Of course, he reaps the benefits by helping to create a better sexual encounter for himself as well as for her.

Some women who experience difficulty reaching orgasm have more general problems "letting go" during sex. They are afraid of losing control to their partners. Or there may be conflicts in the relationship that lead the woman to hold back from orgasm. In these cases, seeking help from a qualified sex therapist seems advisable.

The vagina rebels: vaginismus

Alan came into my office because he was puzzled by the problem he and his girl friend, Beth, were having with sex. Their relationship was relatively new, but they had been involved sexually for several weeks. All of their attempts at intercourse had failed, and Alan blamed the trouble on what he termed Beth's "overly tight vagina." He told me, "She's just too small, and I can't get my penis in."

Since it is rare for a woman's vagina to be malformed or "too tight," this type of complaint usually alerts a sex therapist to the possibility of vaginismus. This is a condition in which the outer vaginal muscles become tense whenever an effort is made to insert anything into the vagina. They become taut enough actually to prevent intercourse, or at least to make entry of the penis extremely uncomfortable for the woman and difficult for her partner. It's as if the vagina were rebelling and refusing to participate in sex, even though the woman may feel sexually aroused and want to have intercourse.

My first step in talking with Alan was to suggest that Beth accompany him on his next visit, which she did. She confirmed that this had represented a continuing problem for her sex life. She also described some of the fear and discomfort she had experienced during her first attempt at intercourse when she was a teenager. There had been some pain and bleeding because of the rupturing of her hymen, and this had created a negative atmosphere about the entire experience. She never again had sex with that first boy friend, but when she tried intercourse about a year later, her fear was reflected in the tensing of her vagina. Every attempt at intercourse that followed was unsuccessful. Beth had decided there wasn't much to be done until Alan took steps to work on the problem.

After a thorough physical examination, the physician to whom I referred Beth indicated that there were no physical abnormalities. Beth's vaginismus was clearly the result of her inability to relax during sex, so I involved her and Alan in a step-by-step program to improve their sexual life.

The exercises they did together were designed to help Beth relax with sex and gradually to enable Alan to insert his little finger into her vagina. Then over a period of days, as she became more comfortable with that, they began to use his index finger, then two fingers, and eventually his erect penis. At each stage of the exercises, Beth had complete control and was free to withdraw his finger or penis from her vagina whenever she wished. This helped her to feel that she could end any activity that was becoming painful or uncomfortable. By the end of the therapy process, they were fully able to enjoy sexual intercourse together without any trouble.

Again, Alan and Beth's success in overcoming her vaginismus had a lot to do with his willingness to be an understanding partner, ready to work toward improvement of a sexual relationship. Communication was an important part of their

progress and the main basis for their wanting to work together in the first place.

WHEN AND HOW TO FIND A
SEX THERAPIST

People with sexual concerns are often hesitant to seek professional help. One man described his two-year debate with
himself before he finally made an appointment with me to
discuss his problem with ejaculatory control. "I suppose the
main thing that held me back was my own embarrassment.
I didn't realize what a common problem it is and I felt like
I was the only guy in the state with it. Besides, the idea of
asking for help from somebody else makes me feel weak—
as if I'm not much of a man if I can't handle my own worries,
especially in sex. So I kept putting it off, expecting that somehow the problem would clear up by itself. It just never did."

Some men are persuaded to see professionals by their partners, although that kind of persuasion doesn't always work.
Several times a year women come alone to my office to discuss
what is obviously a shared sexual problem. When I suggest that
it will be important for their male partners to enter the therapy
process too, many of these women are doubtful that the men
will get involved. Sometimes they're surprised when the male
partner consents to come to the next session, but sometimes
they are quite right: the man refuses. Some men are simply
too proud or too scared to seek help. Some prefer to blame
their partners and completely disown the problem.

A part of being a healthy, sexually fulfilled man is knowing when you've exhausted your own resources. Sometimes
it helps just to talk things out with another human being, pulling thoughts and feelings into a more manageable perspective.
Sometimes you need the objectivity that an outsider can bring
to your situation. And sometimes specific suggestions are in

order that only someone with professional training can give you. Best friends seldom make the best therapists, regardless of how good their intentions might be.

When to find a professional

Usually the best time to get professional help is when you realize you should and feel ready to do it, even if you are nervous about it. In some cases, you should get the help even before you feel ready. There is one important thing to remember, however. You have to want to work on the problem and be willing to expend some energy doing so. No professional person is going to wave a magic wand over your head; you'll still have to do the lion's share of the work.

Check all of the following statements that you believe apply to you and your situation. Any one of them could mean that it would be a good time for you to consider seeing a professional sex counselor or therapist:

_____ I've been worried about this sexual problem for years but never talked with anyone about it.

_____ I've told a few people about my sexual problem, but nothing has helped yet.

_____ I've tried working with the exercises in this book but have not accomplished what I really need to.

_____ I don't want to use a book such as this and think that a face-to-face encounter with a sex therapist is more what I need.

_____ I once tried talking with a counselor or therapist about my concern, but we didn't get anywhere with it.

_____ My partner is the one with the main sexual problem, but nothing I have done seems to have helped.

_____ My partner feels that I have a sexual problem and that she/he would like to visit a sex therapist with me.

_____ As my partner and I try to work on our sexual concern, other problems between us keep getting in the way.

———— Trying to work on the sexual problem so far has only made things worse.

———— I think that my partner and I are in danger of breaking up our relationship over this sexual problem (and possibly others).

What kind of help?

Whenever anyone had a sexual problem, the old advice was always to "see your family doctor." Unfortunately, the family doctor was often the worst person to contact on sexual matters. Medical schools have now begun to prepare medical students more adequately in the area of human sexuality, but physicians rarely have the time to spend with patients that is necessary for dealing with sex-related problems.

The first step in finding professional help is to decide what kind of help you want and need. Obviously, if the problem is related to illness or some organic abnormality, a physician will be the one to see. If there are difficulties to be ironed out in the relationship between you and your partner, or if you are having trouble dealing with certain sex-related feelings and values, you probably will want to seek *sex counseling*. If you're experiencing any kind of functional problems with sex, such as troubles in erection, ejaculation, or reaching orgasm, then *sex therapy* will probably be your best bet. Therapy includes specific exercises for working on functional problems, although it often includes a good deal of counseling as well.

Most workers in the helping professions—counselors, psychologists, psychiatrists, physicians, social workers, and members of the clergy—do their share of sex counseling. Some do sex therapy. Don't be fooled by titles. Just because someone is called doctor, or is labeled a counselor, or calls himself or herself a sex therapist for that matter, doesn't mean that he or she is skilled in helping others with sexual problems.

You might also want to give some thought as to whether you will be seeking help alone or if you will want to involve your partner. Some professionals work only with couples in sex therapy, while others see both couples and individuals. And how much can you pay? Don't get involved until you have been fully informed of the costs involved.

How to find a sex therapist

Finding a sex therapist is easier than knowing whether or not it's the right therapist for you. While some things can be checked out ahead of time by telephone or by asking around, you may not know for sure until you've seen the individual a time or two. Here are some of my recommendations for finding—and deciding whether or not to stay with—a sex therapist:

1. *Locating a professional.* One of the best ways to locate a sex therapist is to ask a professional person you trust to recommend someone. You might even put it this way: "If you were having a sexual problem, whom would *you* go to?" In cities, the yellow pages often carry lists of professionals who specialize in sex therapy. If you are a stranger in the area, or have no one to ask, try calling three or four psychologists or therapists out of the telephone directory and ask whom—in addition to themselves—they would recommend for sex therapy. If a particular name crops up more than once, you may have a winner. Larger teaching hospitals affiliated with medical schools and local mental health clinics often offer sex therapy services as well. Throughout the United States there are sex clinics too, some reputable, some not. Masters and Johnson's Reproductive Biology Research Foundation in St. Louis is the best known of the reputable clinics, but there are many others.

2. *Checking them out.* Most professionals do not object if you call ahead to find out some details, and in some cases the receptionist can give you the answers. Don't expect anyone to give you a diagnosis or suggested treatment by phone, however. In fact, be suspicious of anyone who tries. Asking questions during your initial visit is a good way to get a better feel for the person and how he or she does things. Here are some of the questions you might want to ask:

What does the therapist charge and how often is payment expected? (You might want to check around to see if this is in line with other therapists in your area.)

Does any type of medical insurance cover the costs?

Does the therapist work with individuals or only with couples? (If it applies to your situation, you might want to know if partners must be of the opposite sex.)

What kind of training and background in sex counseling and therapy does the professional person have? (Reputable therapists rarely are insulted by this question.)

Does the therapist work with another therapist (usually of the opposite sex) as a therapy team, or alone? (You might have to decide which arrangement would be best for you and perhaps your partner.)

What kinds of records are kept, and are they treated in a totally confidential manner? For how long following the end of treatment are records kept on file?

What sorts of methods are used, and are they recognized by any professional organization of therapists? (Beware of approaches that seem to have been invented out of thin air.)

Is the therapist appropriately licensed by your state and/or certified by any professional body to practice sex therapy?

Most states do not yet have licensure requirements for sex therapy, but they will be appearing more and more in future years. There are two national professional associations that certify sex therapists who have met their rigid requirements for education, training, and supervised work. These organizations can provide lists of certified sex therapists in various areas of the country, although even this certification is not an absolute guarantee of the therapist's competence. The two associations are:

American Association of Sex Educators, Counselors,
    and Therapists (AASECT)
5010 Wisconsin Ave NW, Suite 304
Washington, D.C. 20016

Eastern Association of Sex Therapy (EAST)
10 East 88th Street
New York, New York 10028

3. *What you're looking for.* You should be able to feel
comfortable and relatively relaxed with your therapist. Look for
the kind of atmosphere in which you are free to discuss things
and express your feelings without being judged, put down, or
made to feel embarrassed. You should sense a degree of trust,
caring, and respect between yourself and the therapist. Ideally
he or she can interact with you as a person as well as being
"The Expert" to whom you came for help. Most importantly,
you're looking for progress. Sex therapy takes time, and you
will need patience, but after a few sessions and some working
on your own, you should be able to feel that something is
happening. Any therapy process has its ups and downs, even
when progress is being made. If you're discouraged, talk about
it with the therapist. If several sessions go by without progress,
or if your therapist is defensive about your discouragement,
maybe it's time to look for help elsewhere.

4. *What you're NOT looking for.* In every profession there
are the incompetents, quacks, and charlatans. Sex therapy has
its share as well. Here are some things to look out for:

> Seductiveness or sexual aggressiveness on the part of
> the therapist.
>
> The suggestion that you and the therapist should be
> nude together. (Some reputable therapists carry on
> physical examinations, although it is legitimate to re-
> quest that this be done by a physician or under a
> physician's supervision.)
>
> Advertisements for the therapist in tabloid newspapers
> or other seemingly unprofessional locations.

Any claim by the therapist that his or her methods are 100 percent effective or superior to all others.

The therapist who is too quick to take over and solve your problems for you, without expecting you to work and take a share of the responsibility.

Suggestions that you try sex secretly with someone other than your spouse or regular sexual partner. (The use of sexual "surrogate" partners has faded away among even the larger sex therapy clinics.)

The therapist who tries to impose his or her values about sex on you, when you do not wish to change your ways of looking at things.

A situation in which confidential information about you is shared with someone else by your therapist in other than an anonymous way unless you have agreed to it. (This could also be grounds for legal action.)

Keep in mind that you are always free to find another therapist. Good professionals understand that they won't be right for every client and are often willing to provide names of other therapists if you're not satisfied. Don't allow yourself to be bullied by any professional.

SEXUAL GADGETRY AND PARTNERSHIPS

The age of technology was bound to notice sex as well as other aspects of life. There are all sorts of gadgets that are designed to improve sex between partners. With the exception of vibrators, which may often be of significant help in generating orgasm, I see sexual gadgets as interesting for sexual experimentation but of little use otherwise. This is not to say that gadgets won't make sex more fun or represent an enjoyable change of pace, because they can. But be careful that gadgets don't become necessary for your sexual satisfaction with a partner. That kind of crutch may be inconvenient, as well as an eventual source of conflict between the two of you.

Sometimes sex gadgets can remove the pressure to perform. I had one male client who was troubled by erection problems. As our therapy proceeded, he discovered that he felt much more relaxed if he had a plastic "erect penis" handy just in case his own didn't work as he wanted. Just the removal of that pressure helped to improve his erections. Gadgets are typically sold as novelties, and often at outrageous prices, compared to the cost of the materials in them. They generally have not been scientifically tested and seldom do what their advertising may claim. Buy sensibly, don't expect miracles, and be careful not to get ripped off. Gadgets are often available in "adult shops," although mail order buying may be less embarrassing. The only trouble is that mail order firms are not always reliable, and jilted customers are usually hesitant to bring their complaints to postal authorities or the Better Business Bureau. In addition, your name may find its way to mailing lists that will bring a deluge of sexually oriented ads to your mailbox.

Vibrators and sleeves

Vibrators come in battery-operated and plug-in models. Some are cylindrical or penis-shaped, in a variety of lengths and widths. Others come with several attachments to be used for stimulating different sex organs and other parts of the body. There are also vibrators that have an attached plastic ring to fit around the penis. Plastic sleeves are available which fit over the cylindrical vibrators, adding contoured shapes and masses of nubby projections. These apparently enhance the stimulating effects of the vibrator, making it more versatile. Of course, no electrical device should be used in the bath or shower.

Sex therapists primarily recommend vibrators for people who are having trouble reaching orgasm, especially women. The rapid vibration is often just the kind of intense, localized stimulation that can trigger a climax. Application of the vibrator to the clitoral area is usually especially effective, although vaginal insertion is enjoyable for many women. Men generally seem less taken with vibrator stimulation than women often are. Direct application of a vibrator to various parts of the penis, especially the head, can be pleasurable for men, however. Occasionally, vibrators can help males who are having trouble with delayed ejaculation.

Vibrators can be used in partnership sex for fun and variety. A vibrator can be made a part of intercourse, adding some extra stimulation wherever it might be needed. Some men like to take a break now and then during sex to prolong the time it takes them to ejaculate. A vibrator may act as a good substitute during a break. The only way to tell if one of these devices can enhance your shared sex is to try one.

Dildos and penis extenders

Cylindrical dildos, made of everything from ivory to clay, have been around for at least twenty-five hundred years. Today, they're usually made of soft, flexible plastics. Although often used for solitary masturbation, a little ingenuity can fit dildos into some interesting partnership sex. As my client discovered, a man who is having erection problems can use a strap-on dildo (also known as "prosthetic penis aid") as a substitute for the erect penis.

There are also plastic penis extenders available which fit over the head of a man's penis, supposedly to make it seem longer during sex. Extenders appeal to men who believe the myth that the longer the penis, the more satisfied the partner. Actually, such devices rarely yield extra pleasure for a partner and may even reduce the sexual sensations for the male.

Rings and things

Some men get a sexual kick out of wearing a metal, rubber, or leather ring around the base of the penis and scrotum. These are usually called "cock rings." Some sex therapists feel that rings and wider bands worn around the penis help to maintain erection, although I do not know of any research to support this contention. If a ring is too tight on the penis, there is some risk of injury to the organ. When worn on the nonerect penis, the only risk is losing the ring down your pant leg. A friend of mine tells the story of the day when the metal ring he enjoyed wearing went clattering across a restaurant floor.

Another variation on the ring theme is the clitoral "tickler." These are worn at the base of the penis and have some sort of projections on the top surface. During intercourse the projections press on the clitoris, providing special stimulation for the female. In view of the fact that many women require clitoral touching to reach orgasm during intercourse, the idea makes sense. I know of some couples who swear by clitoral ticklers, while others find them to be useless. Again, if you and your partner are interested, run your own tests.

A NOTE ON *NOT* MAKING IT TOGETHER

Sometimes two people who have had a relationship together, and who have worked to improve their sexual interactions, eventually must face the truth that they are simply not going to find what they had hoped for in being together. That difficult realization may happen early in a partnership or after many years of being together. The reasons for not being able to make it are as widely varied as human beings themselves.

I recently worked in counseling and sex therapy with a couple who had been married twenty-six years. Craig talked of years of sexual frustration, during which he had found Evelyn unresponsive to his sexual overtures. "I can't go on this way any longer," he said during our first session. "I feel as if there has been a part of me missing and I want it back. I'm almost fifty, and I can't pretend that sex doesn't matter anymore."

Evelyn's point of view was very different, of course, and she told of the constant hurt she had felt over the years at Craig's apparent willingness to give more importance in his life to his career and business friends than to her. "I always was there when he needed me, as I thought a wife should be. I wanted a little tenderness and warmth but never got it. I couldn't just hop into bed and become a fantastic sexual partner when most of the time I was feeling hurt and used."

Their situation had become a vicious circle of misunderstanding and resentment. Meaningful communication was nearly nonexistent. As we tried to work through the mess, both Evelyn and Craig gradually came to the conclusion that in many areas, including sex, their needs were very different. They also realized that neither one of them had much motivation to change either themselves or the relationship. Reluctantly, and with much pain, they chose to separate.

When relationships don't work, it is not unusual for one or both partners to have a sense of failure. Questions get asked such as "Where did I go wrong?" "What more could I have done?" If the breakup involves sexual incompatibility, one partner may leave the relationship feeling undesirable and sexually inadequate. One of my clients found out that his wife of ten years was having an affair with another man and wanted out of their marriage. The thing that concerned him most, however, was his wife's admission that she had never found him to be an adequate sexual partner who could satisfy her needs in bed. Unfortunately, instead of telling him in the early stages of the relationship, she let her dissatisfaction grow inside until she was drawn away from him by a better bed partner for her. Their marriage ended too. The husband was left not only with his sense of loss, but with a gnawing feeling of having fooled himself for ten years about his sexual prowess. After working with several exercises from this book, talking out his feelings, and finally finding a new sexual partner, he was able to feel good about himself again as a sexual male.

If you come to the point in a partnership when you both feel you have done all you wish to do to stay together and decide to split, try to focus away from establishing who was at fault. Nearly always, both partners must share the responsibility for what happens to a relationship, positively as well as negatively. You can instead turn your energies to the future and how to make it better through what you have learned from your past.

Not all couples can find sexual happiness together, any more than they can find satisfaction in nonsexual ways totally. When problems develop, or you begin to be able to admit that problems are already present, find out what ways you can work on them. The real foundation for success must be a mutual willingness to work together toward the improvement of sex. That will always involve caring and compromise. You may never get to the point where your sexual fantasies take you, but the chances are good that you can find a level of sexual interaction that will be mutually satisfactory. If, after working, you find this to be impossible or not enough, then you may have to face the difficult decision of whether or not to stay together. If that happens, you might want to think over your answers to the following questions:

> Now, what do I really want from my sexual life?
>
> What things about the sexual partner I'm leaving were the most desirable and enjoyable?
>
> What things were the most undesirable and interfered with my sexual enjoyment or satisfaction?
>
> Before finding another partner, what aspects of my own sexuality should I work on and change?
>
> How will I go about making these changes?
>
> In what ways can I improve on my patterns of communication with a new partner?
>
> How am I feeling about myself, and how much am I blaming myself for our breakup?

8

Fulfilling
Male Sexuality

By the words *brotherhood, fatherhood, husbandhood,* society describes the way a man is supposed to act, feel, and interact with other people. Fortunately, much of the old clout is gone from these labels. Men are gradually becoming more free to be themselves. Having this freedom means there are new choices to be made and new responsibilities to be taken. All have implications for male sexuality.

BROTHERHOOD

A man is lucky if he has even one really close male friend, someone to share hopes, dreams, fears, and feelings with. That kind of brotherhood comes along during teenage years, but later on male competition establishes blocks that prevent friendships between men. When he was going through a particularly rough time in his life, Brent came to me for counseling. We developed a close relationship, and he talked with me easily about some of his deepest feelings and needs. His life was back in order shortly, but he seemed hesitant to end the counseling relationship. Finally, I confronted him with my belief that he no longer needed counseling. "I know that," he admitted, "but I don't have anybody else to talk to, and I don't want to give up something that feels so good. I'd forgotten what it was like to have a good friend."

Men's relationships seem always to be walking a thin line between what is "appropriate" and what is not. Brent described it this way: "There is always a level of tension between me and other men. I can't just relax and let my barriers down. I'm too conscious of not wanting to do or say anything that would make me look weak, stupid, or as if I'm being taken. And I'm afraid if I try to show another man that I like him and want his friendship, he'll think I'm gay."

Relating to other men: a questionnaire for males

This questionnaire can help you, as a male, to assess how you relate to other men. According to the following scale, give a rating of how you tend to act now, and how you would prefer to be able to act, for each statement:

RATING SCALE: 5 = Almost all of the time
4 = More often than not
3 = Occasionally
2 = Rarely
1 = Never

How I act now	How I would prefer to act	Ways I behave around another man (or other men)
————	————	Talk about business and money matters.
————	————	Talk about sports and competition.
————	————	Feel able to share sadness and depression.
————	————	Joke about sex in a general way.
————	————	Feel able to discuss my own sex life.

		Discuss a sexual problem I might be having.
_____	_____	Get very silly and "childish."
_____	_____	Tend to brag and exaggerate things a bit out of proportion.
_____	_____	Share my deepest feelings.
_____	_____	Talk about women.
_____	_____	Talk about my house, car, or other material possessions.
_____	_____	Feel somewhat tense and unrelaxed.
_____	_____	Discuss problems in my life that are bothering me.
_____	_____	Confide parts of myself that I won't tell just anyone.
_____	_____	Feel more comfortable and accepted than I do with a woman (or women).

Take time to look back over your ratings, especially those where numbers in the two columns are different. Is there anything you could do to change in the direction you seem to want? Why is it that you act in the ways you do around other men? Also try answering these additional questions:

Do you have one or more male friends whom you consider to be especially close and with whom you would share anything about yourself?

Do you feel uncomfortable about expressing affection to other men, and if so, why?

Who is the closest male friend you have, and what is it about him and your relationship that makes him so?

Someone commented once that you can tell basketball is largely an American game because players get penalized for touching each other. Touching between men is generally limited to handshakes that do not linger, quick jabs to the upper arm, brusque pats on the shoulder, and slaps to the backside. And there are only certain times when even these touches are acceptable, such as meeting each other after an absence, after telling a joke, or during sports events. It is seldom that one man reaches out deliberately, slowly, and gently to touch another man as an expression of warm, positive emotions.

One of my male clients sat directly in front of me, talking over some painful details of his recent life. It occurred to me that our session together should be filled with emotion, and yet we were both very calm and collected. I could feel the tension welling up inside me and guessed that he might be feeling the same. Finally, I gulped once and extended my hand toward him, asking if I might take his hand to show that I was with him. He reached forward gratefully, and as soon as my hand clasped his, he began to sob. Tears rolled down his cheeks. He continued to talk about his life and feelings, but it was as if we had suddenly reached an entirely new level of mutual trust, respect, and caring. It was probably the most constructive session the two of us ever had together, and he explored aspects of his life we had never before touched upon. Yet it is seldom that men take the risk of crossing the no-touch barrier.

My concern is that men's hesitancy to touch one another reflects a lack of acceptance of their own bodies and feelings. Touching is a valid form of human communication, yet males hold back out of the fear that their touch will be misinterpreted as a homosexual gesture, or that the other man may pull away. Yet if you feel good about your body and at peace with your emotions, touching can be a powerful expression of total manhood. And touching certainly does not have to carry with it any sexual meaning at all.

Men can enjoy looking at one another's bodies too, partly for comparison, partly out of admiration. Sometimes there is surely some sexual arousal connected with the looking, and that is a natural, expectable aspect of being human. In locker rooms there is a difficult-to-describe camaraderie of nudity. It is as if some barriers are let down when clothes come off. There is always a tentativeness in the looking, lest it be misinterpreted as "queer," but it is part of the locker room atmosphere that many men enjoy.

These are the body intimacies that men are permitted and take advantage of, all a part of brotherhood. One young man told me about one of his favorite parts of camping out with his friends. "There is nothing better than standing around with a group of guys, everybody pissing together. I really feel a part of things then, and as if these guys are really my friends." Another example of how body brotherhood is permitted.

How do you feel about touching and looking at other men's bodies? The following questions can help you decide:

1. When was the last time you remember touching another man, other than shaking hands?
   a. How did you touch him and who was the man?
   b. What were you trying to express with your touch? Do you think your message was received?
   c. Were you a little tense and uncomfortable about making such a gesture? Why?

2. Can you remember a time when another man's touch made you somehow uncomfortable? If so, answer the following:
   a. What did you think the man was trying to accomplish by touching you?
   b. How did you respond to the touch?
   c. As you look back on the experience, do you wish you had responded differently? If so, in what way?

3. Can you recall a time when another man's touch felt good to you in some way? If so, continue answering:
   a. Who was the man and what was the occasion?
   b. What need(s) did his touch fulfill in you at the time?

4. Are there any ways in which you wish you could become more comfortable with touching other men? In what ways?

Touching and looking, between men, can be an important part of brotherhood. Your body is one of the main things you bring to any contact with another person. Your emotions are often best expressed through your body. Try not to deny your body as a part of your human interactions.

Brotherly love

Men have an unfortunate difficulty in expressing affection for one another. Mark was describing some conflicts that had developed between him and his best friend. "He's gotten so defensive about everything that I can't seem to talk to him anymore. I don't understand it either; the guy knows I love him."

"Are you certain he knows that?" I asked.

"It's not one of those things we have to say to each other. It's understood."

Assuming that another person knows how you feel is one of the most dangerous traps of human communication. In fact, in counseling I am impressed with how seldom two people really do understand how each other feels. Mark did care deeply for his friend but had never bothered to express that openly. You don't even have to use a word like *love*, even though it is often appropriate. Brotherly love can be an enjoyable and worthwhile part of manhood.

FATHERHOOD

Almost all men produce billions of microscopic sperm cells in their testicles, each one capable of making a woman pregnant. That represents biological fatherhood but has little to do with the process of being a father to a child. Even men who cannot impregnate women, for one biological reason or another, still have the potential for fathering. For men who choose to be fathers, there are many connections between fatherhood and sex.

Being pregnant and being sexual

Most men feel some sense of satisfaction when a partner becomes pregnant. For some, it is a fulfillment of a part of their manhood. A man does not have to be a father but must make intelligent choices about whether or not he wants to be one. And a man who chooses fatherhood should know what pregnancy is going to be like for him and his partner.

Phil was talking with a group of men about his new baby son, when he reminisced about the pregnancy. "I got sick of people always asking if my *wife* was pregnant and how *she* was feeling. I was just supposed to stand back and be the proud papa. Well, I went through that pregnancy too, and even though I didn't have all of the physical symptoms to contend with, I had my share of new feelings and inconveniences. Eventually, I started telling people that *we* were pregnant, instead of that she was. After all, it was something we chose to share, and I was a part of it." Pregnant women experience wide swings of mood, ranging from joy over the pregnancy to feeling helpless, trapped, and depressed. Their partners not only have to adapt to the women's changeable moods, but also experience a full range of positive and negative feelings themselves.

Phil also talked about some of the puzzling emotions he had experienced during the pregnancy. "Sometimes I just didn't feel much of anything about having a baby. I thought I should be excited, but it was as if I really didn't care much at all. Then I would feel guilty about feeling that way. Finally I talked it over with my wife, and she admitted having the same kinds of feelings." It is not at all unusual for expectant fathers and mothers to question the strange emotions they feel, even though all of them are perfectly natural and expectable.

Sex is a major concern for many couples during pregnancy. Once a man learns that his sexual partner is pregnant, he may fear that sexual activity will in some way injure the baby. I had one male client who began experiencing erectile difficulty immediately after learning of his wife's pregnancy, and it took plenty of reassurance to ease his mind and get him sexually functional again. In most cases there does not need to be any restriction on sexual activity during pregnancy. There are a few conditions that cause physicians to require a temporary halting of a couple's intercourse activities, but other forms of sex are often permissible anyway. Some doctors suggest limiting sex during the final month.

In the usual pregnancy, sex does not harm the developing baby in any way or increase the chances of miscarriage. There may be changes in both partners' levels of interest in sex, however. Pregnant women may go through periods of time when they feel much less than their usual level of interest in sex, and other times when they are more interested than usual. Their bodies are going through profound changes that make themselves known in sexual feelings. Men have some of these sexual mood swings during pregnancy too. Some men no longer find their pregnant female partners to be attractive as their abdomens begin to swell. This in turn often makes the woman feel unattractive and sexually inadequate. Obviously, it is essential that couples work at having open lines of communication during pregnancy so all of the new and unpredictable emotions can be discussed together.

Pregnancy can take on special sexual meanings in the more total sense of the word *sexuality*. Man and woman may share a special sense of warmth and closeness and may have deepened feelings of dependence on one another.

You recognize that your bodies have created something unique together, and you may want to touch each other in gentle, stroking, nonsexual ways. There is the thrill of feeling your baby moving around and kicking inside the woman's body. Experiencing these aspects of pregnancy together can be an unusually pleasurable part of a man's sexual experiencing.

You and the male doctor

Most obstetricians, and in fact most physicians, are male. Some men have difficulty dealing with the feelings that arise when they think of a male doctor touching and examining their female partners' bodies. Yet, it is important for a man to learn more about pregnancy and the birth process and to visit the physician with his partner. You and your partner may have specific things to ask about and request. In some cases and as unfair as it seems, the male doctor will be more apt to listen and respond to you as another man than he will to the female patient. So you can be an integral part of helping your baby to be born in as healthy and safe a way as possible.

Go with your pregnant partner to the doctor whenever you can. The physician will probably allow you to stay in the examining room during any internal examination. For this, the doctor will put on a rubber glove and, using a lubricant, will then insert two fingers into the woman's vagina. Another hand will press down on her abdomen. This enables the doctor to detect changes in the uterus and tell a great deal about the baby's growth. You may feel a little uncomfortable seeing another man sharing such an intimacy with your partner, but you can rest assured that it is not very sexy for either of them.

If you have taken the time to understand pregnancy and birth, you should feel free to ask the doctor why a particular procedure is to be done, or request something different. When serious doubts arise, you might want to consider getting an opinion from another physician, which is your right.

Participating in the birth of your baby

Traditionally, men have had little to do with the birth process. Since birth was seen as a scary, painful ordeal for the woman that no man really cared to watch, most men seemed contented with their lack of involvement. Fortunately, this no longer has to be the case. Men may now be active participants in getting ready for birth and in the actual birth of the child. The most widely accepted way is through prepared childbirth classes, sometimes called the Lamaze method.

These classes begin in the latter weeks of pregnancy, and typically several couples are present. There are films showing childbirth, lectures on the birth process, and instructions in how the man can help during labor and birth. There are simple relaxation and breathing exercises that can help a woman work with her body in labor, and the man learns how to be a useful "coach" for her. In the final stages of birth, the woman pushes the baby out through the vagina, and again the man can help with proper coaching. Some physicians perform an episiotomy at the time of delivery, cutting the outer part of the vagina to prevent irregular tearing of the tissues.

In prepared childbirth classes, men often share their fears that they will faint or get sick in the delivery room. Birth is a messy process, and usually there is some bleeding. However, through these classes men end up feeling prepared, and I have never known a man who was sorry he got involved. I know from personal experience the excitement and joy of watching your own baby come into the world. There is nothing to match the experience. Typically, women who have had their partners present as coaches indicate that they can't imagine having done it alone.

Another advantage of being present during the birth is that you witness your child's first minutes and hours of visual awareness. Researchers report that a critical period of "bonding" happens in the first three hours after birth. A newborn baby is extremely alert during this period and will gaze intently at its parents' faces. We now know that an adequate chance for bonding between the baby and its mother and father can be significant in creating a kind of security and contentedness.

Hospital rules and the medical profession can be slow to change. You may have to search for a physician who will co-operate with you in your desire to participate in the birth of your child, a right that should belong to any father. Prepared childbirth classes are becoming more available in most areas, so ask the physician to put you in touch with a qualified teacher.

Your role in pregnancy doesn't stop after your sperm have been deposited in a woman's vagina. The ups and downs of pregnancy are yours to share, and you can be an integral part of the baby's birth. These represent the full exercising of male sexuality.

Sex after birth

For the first two or three days after a baby is born, both parents are usually feeling very high. After the baby is home and some of the harsh realities of parenthood begin to set in, both usually begin to experience some lows as well. Lots of fathers begin making themselves scarce during this period and find plenty of excuses to be away from home. Typically, nobody's sexual interests are running very high either. Doctors usually recommend that couples abstain from sexual intercourse for four to six weeks following childbirth, although there is a fair amount of evidence to indicate that most couples don't wait much longer than three weeks.

It's not at all unusual for some problems to crop up as they re-establish their sexual relationship. The woman's body is still in the process of returning to normal, and she may find sex uncomfortable. The man may notice slight changes in her anatomy. Both of them are probably under stress from having a new baby around, and fatigued from their new chores. Not exactly the best conditions for great sex. Additionally, some women find a dramatic decrease in their sexual interests for a few weeks or months after giving birth. This can be alarming to both partners, and gentle understanding is called for. She needs to be reassured that gradually she will feel her familiar sexual needs returning, and things will seem more back to normal sexually.

The first three or four months after having a baby are stressful ones for nearly all couples, and good communication is essential for staying on an even keel.

Being a father

You will have to work out with your partner a fair division of the "crap work" of parenthood. At first, there are diapers to be changed, baths to be given, clothes to be washed, and loads of other duties. Fatherhood means sharing in these ways of gaining a better understanding of your child. The jobs never stop. As children grow, their needs change, but there are always things to be done.

One essential for being a good father is effective communication between you and your children. Your body and your sexuality are a part of fatherhood too. Babies and children get messages from the way you touch and hold them. They can feel your skin and muscles, see the expressions in your face, and smell the distinctive odors of your body. Before they know you through your words, they will know you through your body. As they grow older, it is not unusual for children to have some sexual fantasies about their fathers and to feel some occasional sexual arousal for them. You may sometimes find that physical closeness with your child also generates a degree of arousal in you. Although men report feeling guilty about such sensations, they are probably very common and certainly do not mean that you are going to have any sexual contact with the child.

During a recent period when my wife was taking courses in the mornings, I was caring for our baby every day. One day, I drove up to the drive-in window at the bank with the baby in her car seat. The woman at the window greeted me cheerily, "I see you're baby-sitting this morning." In reality, I never baby-sit with my own child; I was just being a father. And yet because I am a man, people think it remarkable that I am good at taking care of a baby, and they think that my wife is lucky to have such help.

Looking at fatherhood: a questionnaire

Most often, stereotypes of what a father ought to be get in a man's way, preventing him from just being one. Here is a list of some of the qualities attributed to fathers. Some represent stereotypes, although they may also be qualities of very good fathers. Others are not as often associated with fatherhood. Rate each quality according to your opinion, using the following rating scale:

> IN MY OPINION, THIS QUALITY IS:
> 5 = Essential to being a good father
> 4 = Important to fatherhood but not essential

3 = Desirable in fathers, but not especially important
2 = Undesirable in fathers
1 = Detrimental to good fatherhood

_____ Being a strong disciplinarian
_____ Fairness
_____ Willingness to admit mistakes
_____ Good provider
_____ Keeping emotions under rigid control
_____ Strictness in setting and enforcing rules
_____ Gentleness
_____ Ability to express emotions openly
_____ Intelligence
_____ Has love and respect for children's mother
_____ Physically strong
_____ Interest in athletics
_____ Warmth and sensitivity
_____ Trust in the goodness of his child(ren)
_____ Strong sense of responsibility
_____ Shares in kitchen duties and housework
_____ Strongly believes in honesty and decency
_____ Enjoys playing with his children
_____ Always able to "make things right"
_____ Ability to show that he's not perfect
_____ Spends as much time with his children as their mother does

When you have finished rating each quality, examine your ratings. Pay particular attention to those characteristics you rated with a 4 or 5. Finally, think about your answers to the following questions:

1. Are there any qualities you would want to add to the list as particularly desirable or undesirable in fathers?

2. Think about some fathers you know. Which of them, in your opinion, are best? What qualities do they possess that make them so?

3. How well did your own father live up to the image of good fatherhood that you have in your mind?

4. If you are a father yourself, how well are you meeting your own goals for good fatherhood? If you are not particularly satisfied with how you are doing, in what ways would you like to be able to change?

5. If you are not a father, but anticipate being one some day, what qualities do you most want to have? (You might enjoy talking this over with another man or a woman.)

Fatherhood and sex education

Education in human sexuality is far more than talking about the facts of life or answering the child's question "Where do babies come from?" From the day a child is born, the ways it is named, dressed, handled, and loved, the toys it is given to play with, and the ways it sees adults interacting with one another are all important parts of its sex education. A father plays an important role in the entire process. As a father, you can show your child how to be loving and considerate of others. Your skills at communicating ideas and expressing feelings will be copied and learned by your child. Later on, these qualities may be important to your child's own sexual happiness.

Parents sometimes ask for my advice concerning nudity and children. Should you be naked in front of your kids? Should you allow them to be naked around the house? At what age do you put an end to the nudity? My usual recommendation is to do whatever seems comfortable and natural for you without pushing your children one way or the other. If you feel okay in the nude around your kids, they'll feel okay too. You may find that at various stages in their development, however, they will choose not to be nude around you too. There is no evidence that nudity is at all harmful, and it may indeed help children to feel comfortable about their own bodies.

Of course, nudity invites questions. Children ask about your sex organs and what they're for. They may want to touch them. Again, the important thing is to know what you feel comfortable with. If a boy is not circumcised, but his father is, or vice versa, the son may want a good explanation for why he is different. A boy may also wonder if his penis will ever be as big as Dad's. This is not only a good opportunity for some reassurance, but a chance to explain the unimportance of penis size anyway. Girls can learn about male anatomy by seeing their fathers nude. One of my students once wrote in an essay, "I wish my father had not been so afraid to be naked in my presence. By the time I started going with my husband, I really didn't know much about penises and testes. For one thing, I had always believed that a man's penis was much larger in its nonerect state than it really is. When I was a teen-ager, I only saw boys' penises when they were turned on, so I assumed that penises were always five or six inches long and sort of hard. They used to scare me. If Dad could have let me in on his big secret, it could have saved me months of worry."

When it comes to answering actual questions about sex, many fathers leave it to Mom. Both mothers and fathers have unique things to share with their kids about sex, and youngsters need both points of view. That doesn't mean that you have to share details of your own sex life, because you have a right to privacy just as your children do. Parents are often afraid of botching up the job of sex education. As one father put it, "I'm afraid I'll look nervous and embarrassed, and I don't want to convey that kind of attitude about sex to my son." That was a wise decision, but he missed the boat in not realizing that he could do some reading and practicing to get more prepared for the job.

Good sex education is an on-going process, not a one-time shot. There must be a chance for questions whenever they arise. But it doesn't do any good to tell your kids that they can ask questions any time they want unless you are showing them day to day that you will answer questions honestly, accurately, and without undue embarrassment.

As a father, you will be an important source of information and modeling for your kids' understanding of male sexuality. You can give your point of view as a man. This is a significant part of fatherhood for a man, and the following questionnaire can help you think through what sorts of things you would want your child(ren) to know regarding sex. You are one of the main persons to convey to each of your children sexual values and information.

1. Here is a list of issues on which there are wide differences in opinion and values among people. Although you will never be able to ensure that your children will grow up feeling exactly the way you do about these issues, it will be important for them to understand where you stand. Think each issue through carefully.

    a. Is masturbation a normal, acceptable form of sexual behavior?

    b. Should children be brought up with positive feelings concerning their bodies and sex organs?

    c. Should males have more freedom for sexual experimentation and sex before marriage than women?

    d. Is homosexuality some sort of sickness, or just an alternate sexual life-style?

    e. Is sexual intercourse before marriage acceptable under any conditions? What conditions?

    f. Should couples be permitted to have temporary "trial" marriages before entering into more lasting commitments?

    g. Is sexual slang acceptable to you (words such as *fuck*, *cock*, *cunt*, etc.)?

    h. Should pornographic materials be available to anyone who wants to obtain them?

    i. Should prostitution be decriminalized?

    j. Should unmarried teenagers have access to birth control information and supplies? With or without parental consent?

    k. Should treatment for venereal disease be available to young people without parental consent?

    l. Should sexual activity only take place between people who love each other?

2. A father who is well prepared will want to have enough accurate information about human sexuality to answer children's questions. Of course, it will be up to you to decide how much your child is ready to know and understand at different ages. Here is a list of topics that you should be ready to deal with as your child grows. And remember—if you wait for the child to ask you for information, it may well be too late. The questions may never come up. How good is your knowledge of the following areas?

> Male and female sexual anatomy
> How the body responds sexually
> The menstrual cycle
> Reproduction: fertilization, pregnancy, birth
> Sexual intercourse
> Masturbation
> Oral sex
> Homosexuality
> Birth control and abortion
> Erections and nocturnal emissions
> Laws regarding sexual behavior
> Transvestism and transsexualism
> Sadomasochism
> Other forms of sexual behavior
> Sexual customs in other cultures

If you feel that you could use more information on any of these topics, there are a number of books on human sexuality that could help. There are also books available for children and teenagers that could be of significant help with the sex education of your children. See the book list on page 235.

3. Spend some time thinking back on your own sex education, and particularly consider how it could have been improved.

Above all, fathers need to be able to show love to their children. Some men fear that expressing love will make sons into sissies or be too seductive for daughters, neither of which is true. Children hunger for love from their fathers. They want to see it, feel it, and hear it.

I once asked some graduate students to describe in writing their ideas of what a good father should be and then how well they felt their own fathers had lived up to this ideal. One woman's comments were filled with glowing praise for the strength, intelligence, responsibility, and decency of her father. However, she concluded her essay by saying that her statements were "grounded in a wealth of sadness." She went on to explain that "for all the greatness my Dad possesses, he'll never tell me he loves me. He'll show me with material things or decisions made on my behalf, but he'll never really expose his feelings. My model Dad lacks real emotion. I saw a glimmer of it once, years and years ago, but it has been gone for a long while. I hope my husband never permits that to happen with our kids."

Choosing not to be a father

Whenever you have had sex with a woman, there is a good chance that you were more concerned about trying *not* to be a father than you were to be one. For heterosexual men who do not yet feel ready for fatherhood, one of life's worries is the possibility of a sexual partner becoming pregnant. Any time sexual intercourse takes place with a woman of childbearing age, there is a possibility of pregnancy. Effective birth control methods vastly reduce the risks but never totally eliminate them. The only surefire contraceptive, with absolutely no risk of pregnancy, is avoiding sex altogether.

A man should be fully aware of how to avoid pregnancy until he and his partner are ready to choose it. Some men assume that birth control is the female's responsibility, and it is certainly true that most contraceptive methods are designed for women. However, decisions about which method to use should be shared. There are different rates of effectiveness and different levels of risk for side effects. A sexually responsive and responsible man is well informed on these issues. A very brief summary of various contraceptive methods will be given here, and more thorough information can be found in several books and pamphlets.

First, let me describe one of the not-so-effective methods. The old standby that is still one of the most commonly used is *withdrawal*, pulling the penis out of the vagina prior to ejaculation. The reasons for the unreliability of the method—which *is* better than no method at all—are obvious. Many males cannot exercise the degree of awareness during sex to pull out in time. Even for well-controlled men who don't wait too long, there is the risk that sperm will be present in the clear, Cowper's gland secretion which often seeps out of the penis during sexual arousal, even before ejaculation. It only takes one sperm to do the job.

The other method a man can use is the *condom*, also called a rubber or prophylactic. There are two main types: those made of latex rubber and those made of natural animal membranes, commonly called "skins." Rubbers are available dry and lubricated, and some are textured or ribbed, supposedly to provide more pleasure for the female. They should never be used with a petroleum jelly, such as Vaseline, since it will rapidly deteriorate the latex, causing breakage. Those made of animal membranes transmit body heat more readily and provide more sensitivity. They are considerably more expensive than rubbers, however, and are not very elastic, increasing the risk of their falling off the penis during intercourse.

Condoms are almost always packaged rolled and are meant to be unrolled onto the erect penis. Some rubber condoms have a small nipple at the tip to serve as a semen receptacle, while others do not. In either case, you should pinch about the front half inch of the condom together while unrolling it on your penis, so that a space not filled with air is left at the tip. This provides a good reservoir to collect the semen, so that it does not tend to seep back up and out the opening of the condom. It also helps prevent breakage, one of the main risks of using condoms. The best prevention against breakage is to buy well-known, respected brand names and to store condoms in cool, dry places. Wallets and auto glove compartments are the worst places to keep them. Drugstores often have accessible displays of condoms now, and reliable brands are also available through mail order supply houses. A major advantage of condoms is that they provide protection from venereal disease as well as pregnancy.

The effectiveness of condoms in preventing pregnancy can be increased by the woman's use of a *contraceptive foam or cream*. They contain a sperm-killing chemical. These are available in drugstores and are inserted by applicator into the woman's vagina. A full applicator should be inserted according to package directions just prior to each intercourse. The use of foams and creams without any other contraceptive, such as a condom, carries a greater risk of pregnancy. Applying condoms and foam to one another may be an enjoyable addition to foreplay for heterosexual couples.

The other birth control methods are used by women, but men need to know about their effectiveness and risks. The least reliable is the *rhythm method*, in which the woman's menstrual cycles are charted so that during the times when she is most likely to conceive, intercourse is avoided. Charting and determining the time when the egg will be present in the woman's reproductive system takes care and should be done only after careful instruction by a professional. Some women use the method successfully but most find other methods more satisfactory.

Birth control pills, when taken *without fail* each day at about the same time, are the most effective method of preventing pregnancy. They contain hormone dosages that prevent an egg from being released by the woman's ovaries. The pill, however, also carries considerable risks of physical side effects, although these risks are not as dangerous as those associated with pregnancy. Women who smoke, or who are over forty, probably should not take the pill because of greater risks of trouble. Any unusual body symptoms that develop while a woman is taking the pill should be reported to her physician. Birth control pills for men may eventually hit the market, although market research has shown that many men will be unwilling to take them. In fact, the male pill could be marketed any time, but drug companies feel that it will not be profitable for them because so few men will use them. This is good evidence that probably the majority of men would really rather see their female partners take the birth control responsibilities.

The *diaphragm* is a round rubber cup that the woman inserts into her vagina to cover the opening in the cervix, which allows sperm to enter the uterus. Contraceptive jelly is placed in the diaphragm, and cream should be used in the vagina as well. Together, the diaphragm and chemicals block the sperm from entering the uterus and also kill them. The method is statistically almost as effective as the pill and much safer for the woman. The intrauterine device, or *IUD*, is inserted by a physician or nurse practitioner directly into the uterus. IUDs come in a variety of shapes, and some have metal on them. A short string protrudes out into the vagina so that the woman can check to make certain that the IUD is still in place. Even professionals are not yet fully certain how an IUD prevents pregnancy, but though they are effective some women cannot tolerate them, and their safety record is being increasingly challenged.

During a classroom discussion of birth control methods, one of my male students said, "They're all inconvenient, messy, or both." It's true; birth control is a bother. It takes time, planning, and decision making. Parenthood requires much more, however.

Vasectomy

Both women and men may be sterilized as a permanent way to prevent pregnancy. In women, the fallopian tubes are in some way cut and tied so that the egg and sperm no longer get together. For men, the usual method of sterilization is vasectomy, now usually done during an office visit to a physician. A small cut is made in the upper scrotum, and the physician then locates the vas deferens on each side, the main ducts through which sperm move up to the penis. Each vas is then cut, so that sperm will no longer have their passageway to the outside world. Many physicians refuse to sterilize young men and women who have not yet had children. Their fear is that at some point later in life the people will regret their decision and wish that they could have children.

One of my male clients began having erection problems following his vasectomy. He explained that he felt as if he had somehow lost his manhood, even though vasectomy in no way physically affects a man's sexual functioning. Primarily, he was feeling depressed about "losing something," and this made it difficult for him to get an erection. We spent a couple of sessions talking through his feelings, and I continued to reassure him that his vasectomy would not change his ability to have sex. Before long, his old sexual vitality returned, and he felt relieved at not having to worry any longer about birth control.

Abortion

Vince and Theresa ended up in my office after they had discovered that she was pregnant. Their conflict lay in the different courses of action each of them wanted to take. Because they were not married, and because she did not feel ready for motherhood, Theresa wanted to have an abortion. Vince wanted to marry her and have the baby, and he argued that as the father of the child, he should have the right to veto the abortion. Theresa contended that the fetus was in her body, and that she had the sole right to make the decision about terminating her pregnancy. Two weeks later, and still against Vince's wishes, she had the abortion.

Whether or not to have an abortion is a difficult choice for many couples, but it is nevertheless an available option for pregnant women. Early in pregnancy, abortion is a relatively safe and simple procedure that does not even require an overnight hospital stay. Legally, the man has no right to prevent or require an abortion; it is the woman's decision. Ideally, however, communication channels are open enough between the partners that they can talk things out and make a mutual decision that is the most sensible in view of their situation.

Abortion should never be considered an ordinary method of birth control, but instead as a backup in case your contraceptive method happens to fail.

SELFHOOD

When we get down to the basics, it may be seen that good sex results from being comfortable with oneself. A friend of mine puts it very clearly when he says, "My main goal in life is to live contentedly in my own skin, accomplishing whatever is within my capabilities." That is what selfhood is all about.

As I work with people who have problems, sexually and otherwise, it becomes clear to me that an almost universal root of personal trouble is *alienation*. Most problems are the result of alienation from self, or some degree of alienation from the real world. I'll use examples of sex-related problems to illustrate what I mean.

Sexual self-alienation

Hank believed himself to have one of the dullest sex lives on record, and he complained bitterly to me about his inability to get dates and sexual partners. It didn't take long to see his self-alienation showing through. There were few things about himself that he liked or respected. He thought that his face and body were unattractive, his penis too small, and his personality unappealing. Trying to enter into relationships of any sort with so much built-in alienation was bound to lead to failure. He was hesitant to approach people in the first place, and even when he did, his negative attitudes toward himself were self-defeating. He had little self-confidence and even less self-esteem.

Max let his self-alienation push him into a vicious circle with his sexual problem. He had experienced a couple of instances of erectile difficulty. Instead of accepting them as understandable, temporary results of the immediate situation, he began telling himself that there was something wrong with him and that he was sexually inadequate. Unable to accept what could have been a minor inconvenience, his self-alienation simply generated more tension and anxiety, and consequently more erection problems.

The ways in which males are brought up in our society often foster self-alienation. We typically are not taught to become aware of ourselves and then to understand and accept ourselves as we really are. It all gets back to the tyranny of our manhood scripts.

Here are some of the ways in which men are often alienated from themselves. Think about which of them apply to you and your life:

1. *Alienation from your body.* You may never have been able to feel good about your own body and comfortable in it. Our society gives us some narrow guidelines for what is attractive and sexy that few people really manage to meet. You also may feel guilty about the enjoyment of your own sex organs and the pleasure they give you. Body self-alienation can interfere with the relaxation necessary to fully satisfying sex.

2. *Alienation from your feelings.* This book has continually emphasized the important of being aware of and expressing your feelings. Yet, most men have trouble doing both. I was talking with a man recently who was convinced that his emotions were mostly nonexistent. "I suppose I had some once," he said, "but they've been pushed into the background for so long, I think they are gone for good." He had been experiencing trouble enjoying sex, and everything in his life seemed to lack color and vitality. Men are often not allowed to make emotions a valid part of their lives, and this represents a dangerous form of self-alienation.

3. *Alienation from communication skills.* Babies and chil-

dren communicate spontaneously. Their feelings are evident, and they say whatever happens to be on their minds. It doesn't take long, however, for their communication skills to get stifled. They learn to play the standard games, cover up the truths of situations, and avoid confronting personal problems. Their natural communication skills get buried, and a part of themselves gets lost. This is the area where self-alienation most easily turns into alienation from other people, and this is a sure way of generating sexual problems.

Real-world alienation

Many problems arise out of fighting reality, an inability to accept life as it sometimes must be. One of my sexually frustrated male clients was convinced that "women are all alike," and that he didn't have a chance with them. His problem lay in the fact that once he had established even minimal contact with a woman, he expected her to be faithful to him from that time on. He took one female acquaintance on two dates, and they shared sex the second time. There were no commitments or promises made about the future of their relationship. He followed his usual pattern of falling madly in love immediately. I received a late-night telephone call from him in which he bitterly described how he had found out the woman had recently dated another man. He used his same old lines: "Women are all alike" (meaning they can't be trusted), and "Why is it I always lose everyone I love?" (meaning that he had expected undying loyalty after two dates). The simple fact of the matter is that the real world just doesn't work that way. He was alienated from that reality.

The real world sometimes deals some unfair blows as well. Some relationships don't work, no matter how much work goes into them; people get afflicted with illnesses and injuries that can affect their sex lives; partners fall out of love; and people die. The more alienated you are from these harsher facts of life, the more you set yourself up for trouble. Some things have to be accepted, or you will waste energy fighting a battle that can't be won. The trick is knowing when there is something you can do, and when you have to accept the real world's uncomfortable reality.

Reducing alienation

If you feel that you are somewhat alienated from yourself or from the real world, here are some suggestions that can help:

1. Work at giving yourself permission to be the person you are, with feelings and flaws.

2. Find someone to talk with who can give you an atmosphere of acceptance and not being judged.

3. Work toward accepting that life will not always seem fair and that you will not always get exactly what you want.

4. Make use of body awareness exercises (such as those in Chapter 3 of this book) to bring you back in touch with the sensitivities of your own body.

5. Try to approach other people with openness, giving them a chance to reach you, instead of always being on the defensive.

Sexual selfhood

Achieving selfhood is what man's sexuality is all about. The keys to a full sex life and to preventing sexual problems are in understanding and accepting all parts of oneself and changing those aspects that create tension. Here are some of the qualities for which you will want to strive:

1. An awareness of your body and how it responds to being touched, in its sexual parts and nonsexual ones.

2. An understanding of how your body reacts during sexual arousal, and what types of stimulation are most effective in arousing you.

3. An ability to be aware of and control the rate of your sexual response so that you can create sexual experiences that will be lasting and enjoyable for you and a partner.

4. An understanding that you are an individual with your

own particular sexual needs and preferences. It is for you to judge how good and right these parts of your sexuality are for you and whether or not you will act on them.

5. A degree of self-acceptance that will permit you not always to have to be successful at everything you undertake. That is an unreasonable expectation to place on anyone.

6. An acceptance of your emotions as a central part of your personality, worthy of expression.

7. A willingness to expend energy on communicating real thoughts and feelings to persons who are important to you.

8. An awareness that sometimes you may not be able to handle your own or other people's problems and that seeking outside help will be advisable at these times.

Feeling good

My greatest hope in writing this book has been that men who read and use it will be able to feel good about their sexuality and all the things that are a part of it. Feeling good means that you put aside the aspects of your personality that alienate you from yourself. Learn to enjoy the totality of your body, your feelings, and your connections with other human beings. In short, feel good about being a sexually fulfilled man.

Books on Human Sexuality

The people I see in sex therapy often ask me to recommend books to them. Following are the titles that I feel are good and have something to offer almost everyone.

General books on human sexuality

These books deal with nearly all aspects of human sexuality, including anatomy, behavior, and social factors. Any one of them can help answer many questions (including those from children), and would be wise to keep handy.

Gagnon, J. H. *Human Sexualities*. Glenview, Ill.: Scott, Foresman & Company, 1977.

Katchadourian, H. A., and Lunde, D. T. *Fundamentals of Human Sexuality*. New York: Holt, Rinehart & Winston, 1975.

Kelly, G. F. *Sexuality—The Human Perspective*. Woodbury, N.Y.: Barron's Educational Series, 1979.

McCary, J. L. *Human Sexualtiy*. New York: Van Nostrand Reinhold Company, 1977.

————. *Sexual Myths and Fallacies*. New York: Schocken Books, 1973.

Money, J., and Tucker, P. *Sexual Signatures: On Being a Man or a Woman*. Boston: Little, Brown & Company, 1975.

Weinberg, G. *Society and the Healthy Homosexual*. New York: Doubleday & Co., 1973.

Books on men and male sexuality

Daley, E. A. *Father Feelings*. New York: William Morrow & Co., 1977.

Diagram Group. *Man's Body: An Owner's Manual*. New York: Paddington Press, 1976.

Farrell, W. *The Liberated Man*. New York: Bantam Books, 1975.

Feigan Fasteau, M. *The Male Machine*. New York: Delta Books, 1975.

Goldberg, H. *The Hazards of Being Male*. New York: Nash Publishing, 1976.

McCarthy, B. *What You (Still) Don't Know about Male Sexuality*. New York: Thomas Y. Crowell Company, 1977.

Nichols, J. *Man's Liberation: A New Definition of Masculinity*. Baltimore: Penguin Books, 1975.

Roen, P. R. *Male Sexual Health*. New York: William Morrow & Co., 1974.

Zilbergeld, B. *Male Sexuality*. Boston: Little, Brown & Company, 1978.

Books on women and female sexuality

Barbach, L. G. *For Yourself: The Fulfillment of Female Sexuality*. New York: Doubleday & Co., 1975.

Boston Women's Health Collective. *Our Bodies, Ourselves*. New York: Simon & Schuster, 1976.

Diagram Group. *Woman's Body: An Owner's Manual*. New York: Paddington Press, 1977.

Heiman, J.; LoPiccolo, L.; and LoPiccolo, J. *Becoming Orgasmic: A Sexual Growth Program for Women*. Englewood Cliffs, N.J.: Prentice-Hall, 1976.

Hite, S. *The Hite Report*. New York: Macmillan, 1976.

Marine, G. *A Male Guide to Women's Liberation*. New York: Avon Books, 1972.

Seaman, B. *Free and Female*. New York: Coward, McCann & Geoghegan, 1972.

———, and Seaman, G. *Women and the Crisis in Sex Hormones*. New York: Rawson Associates Publishers, Inc., 1977.

Books on relationships and sex

Masters, W. H., and Johnson, V. E. *The Pleasure Bond*. Boston: Little, Brown & Company, 1974.

Rogers, C. R. *Becoming Partners: Marriage and Its Alternatives*. New York: Delacorte Press, 1972.

Self-help books for couples

Comfort, A. *The Joy of Sex*. New York: Crown Publishers, 1972.

Kass, D. J., and Stauss, F. F. *Sex Therapy at Home*. New York: Simon & Schuster, 1976.

McCarthy, B. W.; Ryan, M.; and Johnson, F. A. *Sexual Awareness: A Practical Approach*. San Francisco: Boyd & Fraser Publishing Company, 1975.

Raley, P. E. *Making Love: How to Be Your Own Sex Therapist*. New York: Dial Press, 1976.

Books for children and teenagers

Andry, A. C., and Schepp, S. *How Babies Are Made*. New York: Time-Life Books, 1970. (Children 3–6)

Bohannan, P. *Love, Sex and Being Human*. New York: Doubleday & Co., 1969. (Teenagers)

Gordon, S., and Gordon, J. *Did the Sun Shine Before You Were Born?* New York: The Third Press, 1974. (Children 3–6)

Johnson, E. W. *Love and Sex in Plain Language*. New York: Bantam Books, 1971. (Younger teenagers)

———. *Sex: Telling It Straight*. New York: Bantam Books, 1971. (Slow-reading teenagers)

Kelly, G. F. *Learning about Sex: The Contemporary Guide for*

Young Adults. Woodbury, N.Y.: Barron's Educational Series, 1977. (Teenagers)

Lieberman, E. J., and Peck, E. *Sex and Birth Control: A Guide for the Young*. New York: Schocken Books, 1975. (Teenagers)

Nilsson, L. *How Was I Born?* New York: Delacorte Press, 1975. (Older children)

Pomeroy, W. B. *Boys and Sex*. New York: Dell Publishing Co., 1971. (Teenagers)

————. *Girls and Sex*. New York: Dell Publishing Co., 1973. (Teenagers)

Schweinitz, K. de. *Growing Up: How We Become Alive, Are Born and Grow*. New York: Collier, 1974. (Younger children)

Index

self-confidence, 154
self-examination, 63–67
selfhood, 229–233
self-reliance, 104–105, 153–154
semen, 65, 74
sensitivity, 18
separation, 204–206
sex after childbearing, 217
sex and pregnancy, 212–214
sex counseling, 18, 121, 197
sex counselor, 156, 159
sex drive, 154
sex educators, 159
    fathers as, 220–224
sex flush, 73
sex therapists, 141, 143, 156, 195–201
sex therapy, 3, 18, 121, 197
sexual arousal, lack of, in women, 188–191
sexual interest, lack of, 154–161
sexual prowess, 139
sexual response, 70–76
shaft
    of clitoris, 186
    of penis, 65
showers, 127
silence, 27, 49
skin, 68–69, 128, 130. *See also* condoms
sleeves, 202–203
solving problems, 39
Spanish fly, 162
sperm, 187
spinal injury, 168
squeeze method, 93–94, 103
Stelazine, 165
stereotypes of fatherhood, 218–219
sterilization, 227–228
stop-start method, 93, 102–104
straightness in manhood, 9
strategies, 28
stroke, 110, 168

surrogates, 201
syphilis, 166–167

talcum, 128
tension, 125
tension building, in sexual response, 71–74
tension releasing, in sexual response, 71, 74–75
testes, 66–67, 73
    undescended, 163
testicles. *See* testes
testosterone, 111
Thorazine, 165
ticklers, 204
tobacco, 81
touching, 67–71, 183–184
    between men, 211–212
tranquilizers, 112, 165
trust, 37, 44–45, 48, 77

understanding, 99
underwear, 161
urethra
    female, 186
    male, 65
urologists, 111
uterus, 186–187, 227

vagina, 85, 108, 138, 148, 186–187, 216
vaginismus, 193–194
Valsalva maneuver, 94–95
values, 47, 222
vas deferens, 227–228
vasectomy, 227
Vaseline, 96, 225
venereal disease (VD), 166–168
vibrators, 127, 137, 201–203
vicious circle effect, 107–108
virginity, 23, 25–26
vitamins, 170